D1062680

COMMUNICATION AND MEANING

SYNTHESE LIBRARY

STUDIES IN EPISTEMOLOGY,
LOGIC, METHODOLOGY, AND PHILOSOPHY OF SCIENCE

VOLUME 168

ANDREW J. I. JONES

Institute for Philosophy, University of Oslo

COMMUNICATION AND MEANING

An Essay in Applied Modal Logic

D. REIDEL PUBLISHING COMPANY

A MEMBER OF THE KLUWER ACADEMIC PUBLISHERS GROUP

DORDRECHT / BOSTON / LANCASTER

Library of Congress Cataloging in Publication Data

Jones, Andrew J. I., 1947–
    Communication and meaning.

    (Synthese library ; v. 168)
    Bibliography: p.
    Includes indexes.
    1.   Communication—Philosophy.   2.   Modality (Logic)
3.   Semantics (Philosophy)   I.   Title.
P90.J66   1983   001.51′01   83–4411
ISBN 90–277–1543–2

Published by D. Reidel Publishing Company,
P.O. Box 17, 3300 AA Dordrecht, Holland.

Sold and distributed in the U.S.A. and Canada
by Kluwer Academic Publishers
190 Old Derby Street, Hingham, MA 02043, U.S.A.

In all other countries, sold and distributed
by Kluwer Academic Publishers Group,
P.O. Box 322, 3300 AH Dordrecht, Holland.

Printed in The Netherlands.

to **SIKKA,**
who usually means what she says

TABLE OF CONTENTS

ACKNOWLEDGEMENTS

My thanks are due to all those who have commented on this essay, or aspects of it, at various stages of its development. In particular, I would like to mention Dr. Wyllis Bandler, Professor Robert Binkley, Mr. Graham Impey, Professor Ragnar Rommetveit, Professor Erik Stenius, Mr. Ged Weare, and the editor's referee; needless to say, none of them is responsible for the ways in which I have chosen to respond to their comments.

Those familiar with the work of Ingmar Pörn will realize how much this essay owes to him, both with respect to some of the formal tools employed and the general line of approach taken. He has been a superb teacher, and a very good colleague and friend; my sincere thanks to him for his advice and criticism, and especially for his encouragement, during the eight years we worked together at the University of Birmingham and since that time.

Thanks are also due to Mrs. Susan Pearce, who typed an earlier version of the essay patiently and expertly, despite being grossly underpaid for the job.

I am indebted to the editor of *Acta Philosophica Fennica*, vol. 32, for permission to reproduce some arguments outlined in Jones (1981). Finally, I am most grateful to the publishers/editors who gave permission for quotations to be made from the following works: *Linguistic Behaviour*, by Jonathan Bennett (Cambridge University Press); *Convention: a Philosophical Study*, by David K. Lewis (Harvard University Press); "Language and Languages", by David K. Lewis, in *Language, Mind and Knowledge, Minnesota Studies in the Philosophy of Science, Vol. VII* (University of Minnesota Press); *Pragmatics of Human Communication*, by Paul Watzlawick, Janet Helmick Beavin and Don D. Jackson (W. W. Norton & Company, Inc.); "The Group Dynamics of Schizophrenia", by Gregory Bateson, in *Chronic Schizophrenia: Explorations in Theory and Treatment*, edited by Lawrence Appleby, Jordan M. Scher and John Cumming (copyright © 1960 by The Free Press, a Division of Macmillan Publishing Co., Inc.); "An Interactional Description of Schizophrenia", by Jay Haley, *Psychiatry* **22**, 1959, (the editor of *Psychiatry*); "A Review of the Double Bind Theory", by Paul Watzlawick, *Family Process* **2**, 1963 and "Some Irreverent Thoughts on Paradox", by Paul F. Dell, *Family Process* **20**, 1981, (the editor of *Family Process*); "Towards a Theory of Schizophrenia", by Gregory Bateson, Don D. Jackson, Jay Haley and John Weakland, *Behavioral Science* **1**, 1956, pp. 251–264, (the editor of *Behavioral Science*); "Development of a Theory: A History of a Research Project", by Jay Haley, Chapter 5 of *Double Bind — the foundation of the communicational approach to the family*, ed. by C. E. Sluzki and D. C. Ransom, Grune & Stratton, 1976, (by permission of Grune & Stratton, Inc.); "A Theory of Play and Fantasy", by Gregory Bateson, in *Psychiatric Research Report, II*, 1955, (American Psychiatric Association, Washington, D.C.).

University of Oslo   A.J.I.J
September, 1982

"I distinguish two topics: first, the description of possible languages or grammars as abstract semantic systems whereby symbols are associated with aspects of the world; and second, the description of the psychological and sociological facts whereby a particular one of these abstract semantic systems is the one used by a person or population. Only confusion comes of mixing these two topics" (Lewis, 1972, p. 170).

"It seems to me that when the human species ate of the fruit of the Tree of Knowledge, it discovered that automatic signs could be turned into signals and emitted with conscious or unconscious purpose. With that discovery, of course, also came the possibility of deceit, and all sorts of other possibilities" (Bateson, 1956, pp. 157–158).

INTRODUCTION

This essay contains material which will hopefully be of interest not only to philosophers, but also to those social scientists whose research concerns the analysis of communication, verbal or non-verbal. Although most of the topics taken up here are central to issues in the philosophy of language, they are, in my opinion, indistinguishable from topics in descriptive social psychology. The essay aims to provide a conceptual framework within which various key aspects of communication can be described, and it presents a formal language, using techniques from modern modal logic, in which such descriptions can themselves be formulated. It is my hope that this framework, or parts of it, might also turn out to be of value in future empirical work.

There are, therefore, essentially two sides to this essay: the development of a framework of concepts, and the construction of a formal language rich enough to express the elements of which that framework is composed.

The first of these two takes its point of departure in the statement quoted from Lewis (1972) on the page preceding this introduction. The distinction drawn there by Lewis is accepted as a working hypothesis, and in one sense this essay may be seen as an attempt to explore some of the consequences of that hypothesis.

It is the second half of Lewis's distinction which is my main concern; as regards the first half, I accept the kind of model which he proposes in his 1972 article for describing a language as an abstract semantic system. There, the leading idea is that to assign a meaning to a syntactically well-formed sentence is to assign truth conditions to that sentence − i.e., it is to specify the conditions under which the sentence is true or false. This is, of course, the dominant feature of modern model-theoretic semantics, which itself has furnished us with the most powerful set of tools currently available for the analysis of meaning. It seems to me to be reasonable to suppose that the idea that all sentences have truth conditions should also be accorded the status of working hypothesis (*cf.* Cooper, 1978, p. 5). With the exception of the treatment of imperatives and other non-indicatives presented in Chapter IV, I shall not be concerned with defending this hypothesis in relation to specific types of sentences; nevertheless, I shall be concerned to argue that the truth-conditional approach is to be preferred to one of the other most influential accounts of meaning – the Gricean theory (Grice, 1957). For the anti-Gricean argument forms a natural part of one of the book's main themes – the formulation of an account of language *use* within which a truth-conditional approach to semantics might be accommodated.

Hence the focus on the second of Lewis's two topics: the problem of characterizing the use of language, of saying what it is for a language to be the (or a) language used by a particular group of people. Chapter I develops a critique of Lewis's own solution to that problem, and presents an alternative theory. The basis of the latter lies in an account of the beliefs agents have in virtue of which it is possible for them to engage in signalling (verbal or non-verbal). In formulating that account, I compare the following kinds of situation: (i) that in which a person *a* observes a regularity in the behaviour of another, *b*, noticing, say, that *b* does certain things only at certain times of the day, and then proceeds to use *b*'s behaviour as a *sign*, indicating the time; (ii) that in which *b* and *a* operate a *signalling* system, and *b* sends signals to *a* about, say, what the time is. The key to my analysis of the difference between situations of types (i) and (ii) lies in the fact that signals, unlike signs (as I define them), involve the possibility of *deceit*. I then try to show how the proper characterization of signalling provides a basis for the description of language use. Those familiar with Lewis (1969) will recognize the strategy followed here, but the end-product turns out to be considerably different from his account and is, I argue, a good deal more flexible.

I point to some crucial differences between signs and signals, but I also suggest that a single account of what meaning is – expressed in terms of truth conditions – applies to both; this, of course, is in keeping with the adoption of the basic hypothesis of model-theoretic semantics. It is here that the disagreement with Grice emerges in full; for at the very heart of Grice's theory of meaning lies the claim that there is a fundamental and complete difference between (what he called) "natural" and "non-natural" meaning. The former is exemplified by "those clouds mean rain", "those spots mean measles", and so on, and thus fall within my category of signs, whereas the latter are exemplified in cases of signalling (verbal or non-verbal). Grice's view was that only the second of these two concepts of meaning is relevant to the semantics of natural languages, and he maintained that non-natural meaning was itself to be analyzed in terms of communicators' *intentions*.

Of course I do not wish to deny the important role of communicators' intentions (and recognition by the audience of those intentions) in the analysis of communication; particularly in Chapter III, but also in parts of Chapters I, IV, V, and VI, I try to identify the part played by such factors. But I also try to indicate the explanatory advantages to be gained by distinguishing rather sharply between the meaning of a signal (to be analyzed in terms of truth conditions) and what a signaller means by employing that signal on a particular occasion (to be analyzed in terms of the signaller's intentions).

In my opinion, the most detailed and sophisticated defence of the Gricean position is to be found in Bennett (1976), and the first part of Chapter V examines some of Bennett's main lines of argument. I there try to indicate *to which kinds* of questions about meaning the Gricean theory − reformulated in terms of Bennett's notion of "intention-dependent evidence" − is really relevant.

Research in the areas of pragmatics and speech act theory has been concerned with a very wide range of issues. If one looks, for example, at the kind of programme for pragmatics presented in Hansson (1974), then it is clear that this essay takes in only parts of the field; for instance, a good deal of work in pragmatics relates to the analysis of indexical expressions in language; but I shall here have little to say about indexicals, or about the ways in which speakers' intentions figure in their use. But having admitted that there are gaps of this kind in the essay, let me also say that I think research to date in pragmatics has tended to ignore the general characterization problem, of saying what it is for a language to be the language of a population, with the obvious exception of Lewis's work; and yet it would seem reasonable to suppose that the form of the solution offered to the characterization problem must set the frame within which to tackle more specific issues in pragmatics, and in the border area between pragmatics and semantics.

The presentation of the formal-logical language, which constitutes the second side of this essay, is given in Chapter II. The details of the syntax and semantics of that language are there described; the language itself is used quite extensively in all of the other chapters. Since I want the essay to be accessible to social scientists, this use of formal techniques is likely to create a problem, because − unfortunately − a course in logic is not usually included in the training of social scientists; although courses in quantitative mathematical methods are a standard part of such training, there tends to be so little emphasis on the importance of issues of typology and taxonomy that qualitative formal methods are often overlooked.

It is possible, however, for the reader to get hold of some of the main ideas here proposed regarding the nature of communication without understanding the details of the semantics of the formal language itself. Up to a point, it is possible to read the logical formulae back into English and treat the formalism as simply a short-hand notation; an Appendix has been prepared, in which there is a summary of the readings of the main operators, and a list of some of the more frequently used formulae. (The reader is asked to note that formulae are numbered in the text by means of the number of the chapter (in Roman numerals) in which they occur, followed by an ordinary digit, the whole being enclosed in parentheses. The different sections of the essay are numbered in the same way, but without the enclosing parentheses.)

However, I want to register some reservations regarding this suggestion; it is useful only up to a point; ordinary language is simply not a sharp enough tool for the precise description of social interaction (*cf.* the discussion in Jones, 1980a), and that is why a formal-logical language is employed. Thus the readings in English of the key modal operators give only an approximate idea of how the modalities are to be interpreted, and no more than that; the full picture is given in terms of the semantical apparatus described in Chapter II. This point is a particularly critical one in relation to the modalities V_a and O_a, which figure centrally in my characterization of signalling and in my definition of the two types of trust which, on my account, play a key role in communication. Here it is vital to grasp the ways in which these two modalities are related to one another and to the belief modality; their English readings give only a rough indication.

The formalism is very much more than a system of notation; it is a *logic* – that is, it provides a means of precise description and, importantly, of systematically investigating the logical relations which may obtain between formulae involved in the description of situations in which communication occurs: relations of implication or inconsistency, for example.

A number of texts are available on modal logic, and so the Appendix also contains a list of some relevant introductory titles. In fact the basic machinery of "possible world" semantics, in terms of which most modern modal logic is presented, is not at all difficult to understand, given a little background knowledge of elementary symbolic logic. The basic semantical ideas are extremely simple.

Apart from its origins in the philosophy of language, and in applied modal logic, this essay arose out of an interest in the literature on so-called "pathological" communication, particularly the research of Bateson and his colleagues, and then particularly the theory of the double bind; hence Chapter VI. The descriptions I read of communication patterns in the families of schizophrenics also added to my conviction that Lewis's account of language use needed revision. These patterns could hardly be said to exhibit a regularity of truthfulness and trust, and they are clearly not confined to interaction within the families of diagnosed schizophrenics, although they perhaps occur more frequently there. Those skilled enough in the art of communication can exploit its potential for deceit, insincerity and evasion in a whole range of ways, and an account of language use should help explain how this is possible.

The chapter on the double bind provided a further opportunity to show the formal-logical tools at work, for the main puzzle about the double bind is just how to characterize the kind of inconsistency, or "untenable situation", which it exhibits; and it also provided the chance to return to a main theme of Chapter I: Bateson saw the need for a solution to the characterization problem for signalling, but I argue that he failed to see the *full* relevance of that issue to the analysis of the double bind, partly because he did not himself solve the characterization problem adequately, and partly because of his (misplaced) emphasis on paradoxes of the Epimenides variety. If I am right, the framework of concepts presented in this essay can put the theory of the double bind, or at least some key aspects of it, on a firmer basis.

CHAPTER I

SIGNS AND SIGNALLING

I.1. LEWIS ON SIGNALLING SYSTEMS

The first three chapters of Lewis (1969) are concerned with conventions in general. In his fourth chapter he turns to a particular class of conventions — those in virtue of which, he claims, certain actions take on the status of signals. Lewis thinks that it is not helpful to begin the analysis of signalling from the observation that actions become signals when we endow them with meanings, for such a move would rely too heavily on our prior, tacit understanding of communication by conventional signalling. The task is to make that understanding more explicit: "So let us describe the phenomenon in other terms and leave meaning to look after itself" (Lewis, 1969, p. 122).

Lewis describes what he takes to be the essential features of a *signalling problem* confronting c, a communicator, and a, the audience. Suppose that when c is confronted by that situation which creates the signalling problem, he has three types of possible signalling actions available to him, o_1, o_2, o_3:

o_1 hanging no lantern;
o_2 hanging one lantern;
o_3 hanging two lanterns.

These signalling actions are correlated one-to-one with three states of affairs, s_1, s_2, s_3:

s_1 the redcoats are not coming;
s_2 the redcoats are coming by land;
s_3 the redcoats are coming by sea.

It is assumed that when the signalling problem is at hand c will observe that one of these states of affairs obtains. There are six ways of setting up the one-to-one function correlating signalling action with observed state of affairs. Each way of setting up the function is called a *contingency plan, Fc, for the communicator c.*

It is further assumed that the audience, when engaged in the signalling problem, will observe one of the signalling actions and that he is to base his consequent action on that observation. That is, he is to set his observation in one-to-one correlation with responses r_1, r_2, r_3 :

r_1 warn of a land attack;

r_2 warn of a sea attack;

r_3 go home and give no warning.

Each way of setting up the function from the set of signalling actions to the set of responses is called a *contingency plan, Fa, for the audience a.*

The features of the signalling problem so far described are assumed to be common knowledge for c and a. It is further supposed that it is common knowledge for them that the communicator, but not the audience, is in a good position to tell which one of the three states of affairs obtains, that the audience can perform the responses, that it matters little to c and a which contingency plans they adopt provided that they achieve the desired dependence of response on observed state of affairs, and that nothing else about their plans and actions within the context of the signalling problem matters as much to them as that they achieve the required coordination between the state of affairs observed to hold and the audience response.

For the signalling problem just described it may be supposed that this desired dependence can be expressed in terms of a one-to-one function F, which takes the set $\{s_1, s_2, s_3\}$ as domain and the set $\{r_1, r_2, r_3\}$ as range, and which is defined as follows:

$$F(s_1) = r_3$$
$$F(s_2) = r_1$$
$$F(s_3) = r_2$$

The desired coordination between communicator's contingency plan and audience's contingency plan is achieved if and only if the relative product Fc/Fa is identical to F.

More generally, Lewis defines a *signalling system for a signalling problem* as follows: the pair (Fc, Fa) is a signalling system for signalling problem SP if and only if it achieves the desired coordination between the communicator's choice of contingency plan and the audience's choice of contingency plan.

More formally, the definition may be summed up as follows: where $\{s_i\}$ is a set of states of affairs, $\{o_k\}$ is a set of signalling actions, $\{r_j\}$ is a set of responses, Fc is a one-to-one function from $\{s_i\}$ to $\{o_k\}$, Fa is a one-to-one function from $\{o_k\}$ to $\{r_j\}$, and F is a one-to-one function from $\{s_i\}$ to $\{r_j\}$, then the pair (Fc, Fa) is a signalling system for the signalling problems SP if and only if $Fc/Fa = F$, assuming that F expresses the *desired* dependence (for the solution of SP) of response on observed state of affairs.

It is a central feature of Lewis's definition of *convention* that a convention is a regularity in the behaviour of the members of some population whereby those members secure a solution to some mutually recognized coordination problem. Thus, for Lewis, a *conventional signalling system* is also thought of as a regularity in behaviour; for suppose the members of some population *P* are involved in a certain signalling problem *SP*; then if (*Fc, Fa*) is a signalling system for *SP*, it is a conventional signalling system if and only if communicators and audiences in *P* regularly implement their respective contingency plans, *Fc* and *Fa*, when confronted by *SP*.

So far the concern has been Lewis's discussion of *two-sided* signalling systems – that is, signalling systems in which the desired coordination is that between signaller and audience. But Lewis believes that nothing new needs to be added in order to cope with what he calls *one-sided* signalling, where coordination is to be achieved either between communicators or between members of the audience.

So, if the basic ingredients are there in the account so far given, the initial question may now be raised again: in virtue of what is it true to say, concerning Lewis signalling systems, that the signals used in them have meanings? After outlining the example about the redcoats, Lewis says this: "I have now described the character of a case of signalling without mentioning the meaning of the signals: that two lanterns meant that the redcoats were coming by sea, or whatever. But nothing important seems to have been left unsaid, so what has been said must somehow imply that the signals have their meanings" (Lewis, 1969, pp. 124–25). But how does what has been said imply this?

When he embarks on his discussion of the meanings of signals (Chapter IV, Section 4, *op. cit.*) Lewis begins by considering a *conventional* signalling system (*Fc, Fa*) for some signalling problem *SP*, according to which the signalling action o is such that $Fc(s) = o$ and $Fa(o) = r$. (Thus, also, $F(s) = r$, where F describes the desired dependence of response on observed state of affairs.) Lewis next makes the following, important remark: "Then we might call o – in general and on any particular occasion on which it is given in conformity to the convention – a *conventional signal that s* holds; and we might say that o *conventionally means that s* holds. For o is evidence that s holds, by virtue of the fact that the communicator acts according to *Fc*, hence by virtue of the convention. Or we might call o a *conventional signal to do r*; and we might say that o *conventionally means to do r*. For o is a good means of getting the audience to do r, by virtue of the fact that the audience acts according to *Fa*, hence by virtue of the convention" (*op. cit.*, pp. 143–144).

We might here be tempted to draw the conclusion that it is the fact that (*Fc, Fa*) is a *conventional* signalling system which grants to any member of the range of *Fc* a meaning. But that would be a mistake; for, as Lewis himself explicitly admits (on p. 147 *op. cit.*), the signals may still be said to have their meanings regardless of whether the signalling system is conventionally adopted. The remark Lewis makes at the beginning of his fourth chapter — to the effect that he is there concerned with those conventions which grant to certain actions the status of signals — should not be misconstrued; it must not be taken to imply that conventional adoption of a signal is a necessary prerequisite for its having a meaning; the role of conventionality in Lewis's account is more subtle than that. What is important, for the case of indicative signals at least, is that it is mutually known by the parties concerned in the *SP* that truthful use of the signals by informed communicators provides evidence that certain states of affairs obtain. Within the signalling system (*Fc, Fa*), *o* means that *s* holds since it is mutually known by *c* and *a* that truthful performance by *c* of *o* provides *a* with evidence that *s* holds; (and Lewis assumes, it will be remembered, that *c* and *a* mutually know that *c* is in a good position to tell whether *s* in fact obtains.) Now it may be that *a* can justify his taking *c*'s performance of *o* as evidence that *s* obtains by reference to the fact, if it is one, that *c* regularly conforms to (*Fc, Fa*) when confronted by *SP* — that is, by reference to the fact that *c* conventionally adopts and implements *Fc* for the signalling problem at hand. But it is not essential that *a* can justify his belief about the evidential status of *o* in this way. *Conventional* adoption of *Fc* is not necessary. For one reason — and this may as well have applied to the example about the redcoats' invasion — it may be that the *SP* is not recurrent. There may be just one occasion on which (*Fc, Fa*) is to be adopted, it having perhaps been agreed in advance by *c* and *a* how their contingency plans would be coordinated on that occasion. Then, when the *SP* arises, it will be mutually known by *c* and *a* that, if *c* is reliably sticking to the plan agreed upon, *c*'s performance of *o* will provide *a* evidence that *s* obtains.

I take it then that what matters, from the point of view of determining whether *o* has meaning, is that *o* is an act the performance of which can provide evidence that a particular state of affairs *s* obtains. An audience may be confident that *o* provides evidence that *s* holds in virtue of his knowledge that *o* has been regularly performed when *s* obtains, but it is not essential that his evidence is grounded in this way.

It might be agreed that conventions do not provide the key to the nature of the meaning of signals, but at the same time maintained that the alternative

suggestions outlined above are also inadequate in as much as they overlook
the intentions which signallers customarily have when they perform signalling
acts. It may be thought that the signals used in the operation of a signalling
system have their meanings only if it is tacitly assumed that the signallers
have certain intentions, and that such assumptions are embedded in the
description of signalling systems.

Before answering this point, it is necessary to spell out a serious defect
in Lewis's account of signalling systems, a defect recognized in both Lewis
(1975) and Bennett (1976), and which both writers have tried to correct.

The inadequacy concerned can be brought out by examining Lewis's
notion of a *discretionary* contingency plan, a notion which he introduces,
in his earlier work, in order to draw the distinction between indicative and
imperative signals (between signals that such-and-such is the case and signals
to do such-and-such; Lewis, 1969, p. 144). Lewis stipulates that if Fa is
discretionary and Fc is not, then the signals are indicative; but if Fc is discretionary and Fa is not, then the signals are imperative. For indicative
signalling this idea works out as follows (further discussion of non-indicatives
follows in Chapter IV, below): if indicative signalling action o is performed,
then no particular sort of response need be required from the audience
a — he must just do whatever he thinks best in the circumstances, perhaps
nothing at all; in that sense Fa is discretionary. The trouble with this account
is that it fails to bring out the substantial kind of coordination between
communicator and audience which is present in successful indicative signalling; for the "circumstances" in the light of which a is meant to do whatever
he thinks best are supposed to be the circumstances which, *according to
the signal given by c*, then obtain; thus a is meant to do whatever he thinks
best in the light of what he *believes, on the basis of c's signal*, to be the case.
The substantial kind of coordination in indicative signalling is that between
state of affairs observed by c and a's *beliefs*; but it is just that which is hidden
under Lewis's notion of a discretionary contingency plan for the audience.

In Lewis (1975) there are some changes introduced to cope with these
problems (although they are not presented via criticism of the earlier use
of the notion of discretionary contingency plans). Following a suggestion
from Bennett, Lewis now proposes that, for the indicative case at least, the
signalling action of c must be seen as providing a not with a practical reason
for acting, but with an epistemic reason for believing. It can be seen now,
quite independently of the discussion of discretionary contingency plans,
that a correction of this type has been required all along: for it hardly seems
reasonable to talk, as Lewis does in the 1969 book, about a signal's *providing*

evidence that a certain state of affairs obtains unless some reference to audience belief can be incorporated within the specification of appropriate audience response. (The trouble was, for Lewis, that he wanted to describe regularities in action, and did not accept that the forming of a belief is an action; *cf.* Lewis, 1969, p. 180 and 1975, pp. 10–11. Bennett has similar qualms and so introduces the term "doings" as what he calls a "term of art": actions performed by an audience as an appropriate response to imperatives are "doings", but so too are "belief-acquisitions" – see Bennett, 1976, p. 178. We may wonder what "terms of art" are, and how they function in science; but, more specifically, we may raise the question why we should be so reluctant to describe an agent's forming a belief – or at least an agent's *deciding that* such-and-such is the case – as an action.)

Suppose that the required sort of correction is made to the description of indicative signalling; it might now be suggested, in opposition to the earlier claims about the nature of the meaning of signals, that it is the fact that *c* can intentionally use his signalling action as a means of achieving coordination, between the state of affairs he observes to hold and *a*'s beliefs about what is the case, which grants to the signals their meanings. It might be thought that the signalling action has a meaning in as much as the signaller, acting in conformity with his contingency plan, performs the action intending thereby to produce in his audience a particular belief. Such a suggestion would be very much in keeping with the Gricean approach to the phenomenon of meaning – see, e.g., Grice (1957) and Bennett (1976). But it should be resisted: for, a communicator's action, carried out in conformity to an indicative signalling system, provides a means for him to coordinate what he observes to be the case with what the audience believes to be the case *because* the signal he uses has its meaning. The intentional action of the communicator does not endow the signal with meaning – on the contrary, it exploits the fact that the signal has its meaning.

Suppose the signals of some indicative signalling system (*Fc, Fa*) are members of the set $\{o_k\}$; (like Lewis, I oscillate between describing the members of this set as signals and describing them as signalling acts, and I see no harm in this from the point of view of the present discussion.) The members of $\{o_k\}$ may be said to have meanings in virtue of the fact that a correlation has been established between the members of $\{o_k\}$ and the members of some set of states of affairs $\{s_i\}$. The established correlation is described by the function *Fc*; it is because the nature of that function *Fc* is mutually known by *c* and *a* that the truthful performance of *o* by *c* (who is assumed to be in a good position to be well informed) provides *a* with evidence that s obtains (where $Fc(s) = o$) and thus with grounds for believing that s. A truthful performance by c of o is simply one which conforms with Fc. But *from the point of view of considering whether o has meaning* it does not matter whether c actually does conform to Fc on any particular occasion of performance of o, it does not matter whether c performs o intending thereby to produce in a the belief that s, and it does not matter whether a actually does form the belief that s on the basis of observing c's performance of o. All that matters is that Fc has been established in such a way that $Fc(s) = o$, so that the truthful performance of o by c *would* provide a with grounds for believing that s holds.

I am stressing this point in an attempt to begin to clarify my position with respect to the relation between the meaning of signals and their use in communication. One key aspect of that position is that it is essentially anti-Gricean (this theme is pursued also in Chapter V) – and in this I believe that I disagree with Lewis neither as regards the meaning of signals in a signalling system nor (as will be evident in due course) as regards the meaning of sentences in a language. As was mentioned in the Introduction, I follow Lewis's distinction – discussed further in Section I.4 – between the specification of a language as an abstract semantic system and the specification of the conditions under which it is true to say that such a language is a language adopted by some population (see the first section of Lewis, 1972). And, as will become clearer later on, according to the first part of this distinction meanings are essentially, for sentences in this case, truth condition determining functions which are comparable in nature to the Fc of a signalling system.

The present chapter is largely concerned with the topic raised in the second part of Lewis's distinction; and on this topic I do wish to register disagreement with Lewis. The nature of the disagreement may perhaps be summarized as follows: were Grice's theory understood not as an analysis of meaning but as an analysis of the structure of communicative acts it would be found to be much too narrow in its range of application. Lewis's specification of the conditions under which a language is a language adopted by a population also exhibits just this narrowness, or so I shall argue.

The claim was made above that signalling acts get their meanings in virtue of established correlations between them and states of affairs. But under what conditions can such correlations be said to be established? This question can be shown to be closely related to Lewis's question about the conditions under which a language is a language of a population. But to try to answer it I first consider a phenomenon much simpler in structure than a Lewis signalling system, and to be called a *sign system*.

I.2. SIGNS AND MEANING

From the very beginning of Lewis's account of signalling c and a are assumed to be not merely agents, but agents occupying certain roles — those of communicator and audience, respectively. Some account of what it is to occupy one of these roles is no doubt implicit in Lewis's description of a signalling system, but in order to keep initial assumptions down to a minimum I shall from now on use agent individual variables simply to range over the class of agent individuals in general. By the time the labels "communicator" and "audience" are reintroduced it will be clear, I hope, why they are appropriate.

I believe that it was said of Kant that he was a man of such regular daily habits that it was possible for the residents of Königsberg to use his movements as a reliable indicator of the time. Let us approach the phenomenon of meaning by considering situations which in some ways resemble this.

Suppose that a has been observing b's movements and has thereby formed the opinion that whenever b takes a walk it is 3 p.m. It is perhaps not just any walk, but a walk taken in certain circumstances which a has noticed occurs at 3 p.m. Perhaps b must be dressed in a certain way, as if prepared for a longish distance, perhaps the weather must be good, and so on. Perhaps a believes that there can be exceptions to the regularity, so that sometimes b appears to be early or late. It might even be that a is mistaken in believing that there is a regularity of this sort in b's behaviour — a may have founded his belief on rather poor grounds. But whether a's grounds are good or bad is immaterial for the moment. Given that a does believe, for one reason or another, that b takes his special walk only at 3 p.m. it may justifiably be claimed that a believes that b's taking his walk is a *sign* that it is 3 p.m.

Introducing aspects of the formal language which will receive full specification in Chapter II, let formulae of the type $B_a p$ be read "a believes that p" and formulae of the type $E_a p$ be read "a brings it about that p". The form of the belief which a has about b's behaviour may be represented by (I.1):

$$(I.1) \qquad B_a((E_b p \cdot Z) \to q).$$

For the case at hand the act of b concerned is his taking a walk; Z is a set of sentences describing the special, attendant circumstances (that b is dressed in a certain way ... and so on) in which b takes his walk; and then the consequent of the conditional is read as "it is 3 p.m.".

I find no good reason to deny that the truth of (I.1) is sufficient for the truth of (I.2):

(I.2)   *a* takes $E_b p$ in circumstances Z as a sign that q.

What *a* has done, in forming belief (I.1), is to correlate the occurrence in
Z of *b*'s walk with the truth of q. It may be said, therefore, that as far as
a is concerned *b*'s taking a walk in these circumstances *means* that q. So I
maintain that (I.1) is also sufficient for the truth of (I.3):

(I.3)   From *a*'s point of view, $E_b p$ occurring in Z means that q.

It is quite possible that *a* has formed a number of other beliefs, of the
same form as that represented by (I.1); he might believe that *b*'s doing
p_1 in Z_1 is a sign that q_1, that *b*'s doing p_2 in Z_2 is a sign that q_2 . . . and so
on. And, of course, it is not essential that *a* only take actions of *b* as signs,
nor that *a* only take actions as signs. So *a* might have a set of beliefs of a
type which would bear certain close resemblances to features of Lewis
indicative signalling systems. For, without assuming anything about how
a might describe what he has done, it can be said that by forming this set of
beliefs *a* has established a correlation between the members of some set
of actions/events and the members of some set of states of affairs. The
sign system he has set up for himself is comparable in certain ways to the
Fc of a Lewis indicative signalling system.

Like Lewis, I wish to maintain that when meanings are given, truth
conditions are assigned; I follow him also in having no hesitation in assigning
truth conditions to actions, indeed to anything which is a sign. Returning
to the first example, *b*'s taking a walk in circumstances Z is true whenever
it occurs at 3 p.m. and false whenever it occurs at some other time. In the
example, these truth conditions attach to *b*'s act only from *a*'s point of view,
for it was assumed to be only from his point of view that the act means that
it is 3 p.m. So another way of describing what *a* has done, when he has
decided that *b*'s taking a walk in Z means that q, is to say that *a* has assigned
truth conditions to the act performed in those circumstances. Again, it
matters not that *a* would be unlikely to describe his decision in this way.

In the discussion of Lewis signalling systems it was noted that the signals
used in the system can be said to have meanings regardless of whether the
system is *conventionally* adopted. There does not *have* to be a regularity in
the behaviour of some group (whereby its members act in conformity to the
signalling system when confronted by an instance of the relevant *SP*) in order
to justify the ascription of meaning to the signals. It follows that an audience
engaged in using a signalling system might be able to justify his taking some
signal *o* as evidence that *s* without appeal to any regularity in the behaviour

of agents who are confronted by the *SP* concerned. This observation has its counterpart within sign systems developed by *a*. Although it might be assumed, for the example concerning *b*'s walk, that *a* would most likely form his belief of type (I.1) on the basis of his seeing an actual regularity in *b*'s behaviour, such an assumption is not essential to determining whether *a* takes *b*'s walk in *Z* to mean that it is three in the afternoon; *a* need not be required to have good grounds; agents are not always rational in their choice of sign systems.

However, it is crucial to note that there is one type of evidence which has been assumed to be unavailable to *a* to provide grounds for his beliefs of type (I.1). I have been assuming so far that *a* has not entered into any sort of arrangement or agreement with *b* according to which, for example, *b* will do certain things only at certain times of the day. I have also assumed that it is not mutually believed by *a* and *b* that *a* might be relying on *b*'s actions as a source of information. I have supposed that there is no mutually recognized coordination problem which *b*'s actions are designed to help solve. These assumptions highlight the differences between sign systems and Lewis indicative signalling systems; *a*'s sign system is an interpersonal affair only in a weak sense, in as much as it involves no mutual awareness and no cooperation between *a* and *b*. Some might prefer to describe the differences in the following way instead: they might point out that there is no inter-personal communication involved in the operation of *a*'s sign system. I have no objection to the claim that sign systems should not be classified as communication systems, so long as we are not tempted, by such classification, to lose sight of the fact that both sign systems and signalling systems involve the ascription of meaning to actions. In particular, if only signalling systems (from this pair) are properly called interpersonal communication systems that should not be taken to imply that two distinct accounts of meaning are required, one for signalling acts and one for signs. I have been suggesting that a uniform account of meaning is applicable; if, for sign systems, attention is confined to signs which are actions, then for both types of system meaning is a matter of correlations between acts and states of affairs. That the *grounds upon which a* will take acts as having meanings will differ, as between sign systems and communication systems properly so-called, I do not dispute.

These remarks point again to anti-Gricean aspects of the position adopted in this essay; communication is one of a range of activities which agents can engage in by using meaning-bearing signs; the activity of communicating does not itself require us to abandon the view that meanings are functions which determine truth conditions.

It may be clear that sign systems are not properly described as communication systems and that Lewis signalling systems are; but there are structures which fall between the two and which exhibit varying degrees of interpersonal awareness and influence. I look at some of these next, with a view to furthering the enquiry into the beliefs agents have in virtue of which some acts are accepted as bearers of meaning. Throughout, the concern will not be to stipulate which types are to be classified as communication systems and which are not, just to describe some types of situation in which signs are put to use.

I.3. SIGN SYSTEMS AND THE POSSIBILITY OF DECEIT

Suppose that a and c are members of a community several of whose members are in a position to observe b's movements and to use them as signs. Things begin to get a little more complex and interesting when the agents find out about one another's sign systems. For example, it may be that a and c have discovered that d has a sign system of this kind, related to b's behaviour; if a and c know the details of the beliefs held by d then they can use b's behaviour as a means of finding out what d believes. Let formulae of the type $K_a p$ be read "a knows that p"; then it may be that:

$$(I.4) \qquad K_a B_d((E_b p \cdot Z) \to q);$$

given that:

$$K_a B_d(p \to q) \to K_a(B_d p \to B_d q),$$

then if (I.5) is true, (I.6) will now follow:

$$(I.5) \qquad K_a B_d(E_b p \cdot Z)$$
$$(I.6) \qquad K_a B_d q.$$

As another example, suppose that:

$$(I.7) \qquad K_c K_a B_d((E_b p \cdot Z) \to q), \quad \text{and that:}$$
$$K_c K_a B_d(p \to q) \to K_c(K_a B_d p \to K_a B_d q), \quad \text{and that:}$$
$$(I.8) \qquad K_c K_a B_d(E_b p \cdot Z);$$

then it follows that (I.9) is true:

$$(I.9) \qquad K_c K_a B_d q.$$

For a different kind of case, suppose that c is not in a good position to observe b's movements, but would like to be informed of them; c discovers that a uses a sign system related to b's actions as a means of regulating his own (a's) behaviour, so that some, at least, of a's actions are performed only if he (a) has such-and-such beliefs about what b is doing; b's actions are perhaps an indicator to a of the state of dealings on the local stock market, and a regulates his activities according to that. So c could now use his knowledge of what a is doing as a sign of what b is doing.

Suppose now that it happens that b's movements are quite extensively used by the members of his community as signs of the time of day. The local clockmaker, a friend of b, mentions to him that business is pretty bad, explaining that he thinks that this has something to do with the rigid nature of b's daily routine. After puzzling for a while, b realizes what the clockmaker meant. Where a is any one of the agents who use b's movements as signs of the time of day, b has now formed beliefs of the following sort:

(I.10) $B_b B_a((E_b p \cdot Z) \to q)$;
(I.11) $B_b B_a((E_b p_1 \cdot Z_1) \to q_1)$;

and so on, where q, q_1, ... describe times of the day. (I.10) says that b believes that a takes b's doing p in circumstances Z as a sign that q.

Then it might also come about that a comes to know or believe truths of type (I.10). Furthermore, it may be that a and b form mutual beliefs about the details of a's sign system so that, where formulae of type $B_{ab}^* p$ are read "a and b mutually (commonly) believe that p", it may be that formulae of type (I.12) are true (here, and elsewhere, in talking about formulae, as when their readings are given, I use the formulae themselves to refer to the formulae):

(I.12) $B_{ab}^* B_a((E_b p \cdot Z) \to q)$.

(Mutual belief will be defined in Chapter II, along with the other modalities.)

(I.12) does not imply that b takes his bringing about p in Z as a sign that q, although that might also be true, i.e., (I.13) might also hold:

(I.13) $B_b((E_b p \cdot Z) \to q)$.

It might be thought that, were (I.13) to be true, that would not tie in well with the intended reading of formulae of type (I.1). However, an agent's taking one of his own actions as a sign that q need not imply that the agent

uses knowledge of the fact that he performs that action as a means of informing himself about whether q obtains. (I.13), for example, may be true just
because b knowingly organizes his life in such a way that he brings about p
in Z only if q obtains, i.e.:

    (I.14) $K_b E_b((E_b p \cdot Z) \to q)$.

It is not impossible, however, for an agent to have a belief of type (I.13)
and to use that belief as a means of informing himself. A person might use
his knowledge of what he is doing as a means of drawing conclusions about
his own mental or physical condition. He might take his own persistent
avoidance of other people as a sign of schizophrenic withdrawal, or his
persistent going to the toilet as a sign of kidney infection. In such cases he
would draw these conclusions on the basis of beliefs of type (I.13), together
with his beliefs about what he was actually doing.

    Of greater interest for present purposes is to see how b's belief of type
(I.10) might figure in a complication of the situations described so far. b
might make that belief a reason for bringing about p in circumstances Z.
To extend our story, perhaps b intends to try to help his friend the clockmaker by misleading the residents concerning the time of day. He might
intend to get a to believe that q, by doing p in circumstances Z, when q
is in fact false.

    In his 1977 book, Pörn shows how descriptions of agents' intentions may
be represented formally with the help of the normative modality Shall.
(See below, Sections II.3 and II.6.) The reading "a intends to bring about
p if q" is assigned to formulae of type (I.15):

    (I.15) $B_a(q \to \text{Shall } E_a p)$.

Such a pattern of analysis may be employed to describe in clearer detail
certain features of b's position in the present example; b intends to bring
it about that a believes that q if he (b) brings about p in circumstances Z;
i.e.:

    (I.16) $B_b((E_b p \cdot Z) \to \text{Shall } E_b B_a q)$.

Since it is supposed that b intends to execute this intention by relying on the
mechanism provided by a's belief (I.1), then b may be assumed to have also
the following intention:

    (I.17) $B_b((E_b p \cdot Z) \to \text{Shall } E_b B_a(E_b p \cdot Z))$.

Perhaps the idea that b is relying on the mechanism of (I.1) may be captured by adding (I.18):

(I.18) $B_b(E_b B_a q \to E_b B_a(E_b p \cdot Z))$.

The situation described here in terms of (essentially) (I.1), (I.10), (I.16), (I.17), and (I.18) could, of course, become even more complex. For example, it could be that a himself believes that (I.10), (I.16), (I.17), and (I.18) all hold; or perhaps he believes just some of them; or perhaps he believes them to be true when they are in fact false. Then again it might be that (I.12) replaces (I.10) and that a and b mutually believe (I.16)–(I.18), in which case there is full mutual awareness between a and b of b's intended exploitation of a's sign system. These would be just a few of the many conceivable cases which can be constructed by varying the assumptions made concerning the extent of the agents' beliefs about one another's beliefs and intentions. What is interesting, of course, is that for some, at least, of these cases it would not be unreasonable to suppose that they are properly described as communication situations.

At this stage it is necessary to re-trace the steps a little, and to review the situation from the point of view of a. Suppose that a bases his belief (I.1) on rational grounds – that he would drop that belief if he thought that there was not reasonable evidence for maintaining it. As soon as he has found out that b believes (I.1) he may have reason to be at least wary. So consider a's situation when he forms the belief (I.19):

(I.19) $B_a B_b B_a((E_b p \cdot Z) \to q)$.

It may be that a has no reasonable grounds for supposing that b's familiarity with this aspect of his (a's) sign system will in any way influence b's behaviour, at least with respect to b's bringing about p in Z. He would not then reasonably believe that b's doing p in Z was a potentially *deceiving* performance. But if – going back to the first example – a believes that b might use his taking a walk in circumstances Z as a means of influencing or manipulating a's beliefs about the time, then a significant new dimension emerges, which is of course of considerable interest from the communicational point of view. Whether or not a could now reasonably continue to take b's taking a walk in circumstances Z as a sign that it was three o'clock would depend on whether a considered b to be *trustworthy*. If a believed that b was not to be trusted – that b might want to try to mislead him – then obviously a would not have grounds for continuing to believe that b's walk in circumstances Z was a sign that it was three o'clock.

(The problems which *a* could have here, concerning the evidence for accepting some act as a sign, might also arise even if what *a* took to be a sign were not the act of some agent, but a so-called natural sign. For, in some cases at least, natural signs can be interfered with, or imitated. Suppose that *a* takes a certain kind of colouration on the bark of a tree to be a sign of disease in the tree. Suppose further that *a* and *b* mutually believe that *a* takes the colouration to be a sign of this sort, and that *a* believes that *b* intends to try to produce in him the belief that some trees are diseased by painting on the appropriate colouration. In these circumstances, *a* could reasonably continue to take the colouration as a sign of disease only to the extent that he believed that *b* could be trusted to paint only those trees which were indeed diseased. To the extent that they can be manipulated or imitated, natural signs are subject to the same types of problems pertaining to trustworthiness as those signs which involve the performance of actions.)

Suppose, then, that *a* believes that *b* is exploiting his (*a*'s) sign system, and that he believes that *b* is not to be trusted. In so far as *a* is concerned to base his belief (I.1) on rational grounds, it would appear that he can no longer take *b*'s walk in circumstances *Z* as a sign that, and as meaning that, it is 3 p.m. Surely, at this point, this part of *a*'s sign system would cease to be of use to him as a means of being informed about the time.

But these comments immediately suggest a way in which, from *a*'s point of view, *b*'s act (in *Z*) could be reinstated as a bearer of meaning; *a* might no longer hold a belief of type (I.1), but he may nevertheless have grounds for believing that if *b* does *p* in *Z*, *and the performance is non-deceiving*, then *q* obtains. If *a* believes that there is no real chance that *b*'s act might be used by *b* as a means of trying to influence *a*'s beliefs, then of course the question of whether his (*b*'s) performance is to be trusted does not arise for *a*; but if *a* *does* believe that *b* might want, occasionally or frequently, to try to mislead him − i.e., that *b* is potentially a deceiver − he might nevertheless *still* have grounds for believing that any *non-deceiving* performance by *b* of the act concerned is a sign that *q*. Now *what* these grounds might be is a further question; it *may* be that the background lies in an arrangement or agreement of some sort between *a* and *b*, but that is surely not the only possibility; however, it is not *this* question I am concerned to answer here (*cf.*, pp. 24–25, below).

If *b*'s performance is non-deceiving, then I shall say that the performance is *optimal* for *a*, in a certain specifiable sense; it is a performance which best meets *a*'s interest in being informed, and therefore, relative to that interest, it is optimal or ideal for *a*. Sentences of the type "it is optimal (ideal) for *a*, relative to his interest in being informed, that *p*" will be represented in the formal language with the help of a deontic modality, relativized to agent individuals; the full account of this modality is given in the next chapter; here it suffices to say that the above sentence will be symbolized by the following formula: $O_a p$.

I shall read formulae of type (I.20):

(I.20) $B_a(((E_b p \cdot Z) \cdot O_a(E_b p \cdot Z)) \to q)$

in the following kind of way: "*a* believes that if *b* does *p* in circumstances *Z*, and *b*'s performance (in *Z*) is non-deceiving (i.e., it is an optimal performance relative to *a*'s interest in being informed), then *q* is the case". I shall also say that the truth of (I.20) is sufficient for the truth of (I.21):

(I.21)   *a* takes non-deceiving performance, in circumstances *Z*, of *b*'s
          act of bringing about *p*, as a sign that *q*.

Furthermore, I shall maintain that (I.21) is sufficient for the truth of (I.22):

(I.22)   *a* believes that *b*'s doing *p* in *Z* means that *q*.

This last step is perhaps the one most likely to cause disagreement; the basic idea here is that *a* takes *b*'s act as meaning that *q* if he *would* take a *non-deceiving* performance of that act as a sign that, or as evidence that, *q*. With one further modification to be introduced shortly, formulae of type (I.20) will figure centrally in my account of interpersonal communication. It seems to me to be a commonplace feature of communication situations, and one which needs to be explained, that an agent may take an act he observes to mean that *q* even though he might not believe that that performance is non-deceiving — and so does not believe that that performance is a sign that, or evidence that, *q*. Here it is important to note that I make the following assumption: the act descriptions which appear in formulae of type (I.20) — and of type (I.1) — are descriptions of particular performances of acts of certain types. But whether or not a particular performance of an act is to be taken as counting as a token of one of these types will be assumed to be independent of consideration of what (if anything) the performer may have intended to do *by means of performing* that act. This assumption goes hand in hand with the fact that I wish to distinguish between the meaning of an act and what the performer means by, or intends to do by, performing it.

However, if we suppose that (I.20) holds, then whether or not *a* takes a particular performance by b of the act of bringing about p in Z as a *non-deceiving* performance *will*, in general, depend (in part) on what a believes b's intentions in performing the act to be. For, as I shall later argue in connection with a more highly developed form of (I.20) — and which I shall refer to as a *rule of information* — whether b's act counts for a as a non-deceiving performance will depend, in part, on whether a takes b's act to be intended as an instance of implementation, or exploitation, by b, of a's belief of type (I.20).

These points may be illustrated by means of the following example: suppose that a believes that any non-deceiving performance by b of b's act of putting his hand out of the right-hand side window of his car (the circumstances being that b is driving along the highway in his car) is a sign that, or evidence that, b is about to turn right. Then I shall say that a takes *any* performance by b of the act of type putting his hand out of the right-hand side window of his car (in those circumstances) as meaning that b is about to turn right, regardless of what a believes b may have intended to do by performing an act of that type, and hence regardless of whether a takes b's act to be an implementation of the rules for traffic signalling. But whether a *also* takes b's act as a sign that, or as evidence that, b is about to turn right will depend on whether a takes b's performance of the act to be non-deceiving: and that, in turn, *will* depend *in part* on what a takes b's intentions to be; (some situations may provide exceptions: see Section III.5).

The distinction between the meaning of an act — in the sense here described — and what an agent intends to do by performing that act is, of course, a central aspect of the anti-Gricean approach adopted in this essay to the question of what meaning is. But it should also be clear that I in no way deny the need to consider agents' intentions in the analysis of communication situations; that should be obvious from examples already used; the role of agents' intentions will be further elaborated in examples to come.

The further modification to the structure of (I.20), to which reference was made on p. 21, may be introduced as follows: suppose that a receives a message from b meaning that q, and that he takes b's performance to be non-deceiving. Must a then believe that q? I think not, since there are two ways in which b's performance may be unreliable for a, only one of which has been covered so far. If a does form the belief that q on the basis of receiving the message from b, his grounds will not be merely that he takes b's act to be non-deceiving; he will also be assuming that the information b has is reliable — i.e., that b himself is reliably informed. Thus I propose to read formulae of the type occurring in the consequent of the embedded conditional of (I.23) as "according to the information available to b, q is true":

(I.23) $B_a((E_bp \cdot Z) \cdot O_a(E_bp \cdot Z)) \rightarrow V_bq)$.

On the basis of believing that, according to the information available to b, q is true, a will form the belief that q if he also assumes that b is reliably informed.

a might believe that, according to the information available to b, q is true, and yet not believe that b believes that q; for it would be possible for a to believe both that b's act (of bringing about p in Z) was non-deceiving and that b was not *sincere*; by this I mean that a might well think that the act b performs is not misleading, relative to the information available to b, although he (a) also believes, or suspects, that b himself does not accept that that information is adequate to justify his (b's) *believing* that q.

Of all the modalities used in this essay, V_a is perhaps the one most easily misunderstood; its reading in English is cumbersome and insufficiently precise. The reader is referred to Chapter II for a detailed presentation of this modality, and is asked particularly to note the way it is there related to the belief and deontic modalities within the semantical model.

Chapter III contains further discussion of trust and sincerity in communication situations.

I take (I.23) to be sufficient for the truth of (I.24):

(I.24) a takes non-deceiving performance, in circumstances Z, of b's act of bringing about p, as a sign that, according to the information available to b, q is true.

I shall also maintain that (I.24) is sufficient for the truth of (I.22). What the act means, from a's point of view, is that q. It means that q because a would take non-deceiving performance of it to be a sign that, according to the information available to b, q is true.

The argument so far has looked at what happens when a believes that performances of some act which has figured in his sign system are potentially deceiving; I have tried to show what it would be for a to believe that b's act means that q even when a does believe that b's performances might be deceiving. The account takes us part way to characterizing what it is that a must believe if he is to accept that some act of b's is a *signal* to him that q; it is a partial account of what it is in virtue of which an act counts as a signal (from b to a). a must have a belief of type (I.23). Among the further features which must be added to this account are the following: b must also believe that the act means that q, a must believe that b believes this, b must believe that a believes that the act means that q . . . and so on. In short, they mutually believe that b's act means that q. I will assume it to be a defining feature of signalling systems, but not of sign systems, that the parties concerned are mutually aware of what the meaning-bearing acts mean. So the focus of attention will now shift to formulae of type (I.25):

$$(I.25) \quad B^*_{ab}(((E_b p \cdot Z) \cdot O_a(E_b p \cdot Z)) \to V_b q)$$

I shall refer to (I.25) as a *rule of information* (for a and b, relative to b's bringing about p in circumstances Z).

At the end of Section I.1 the question was raised concerning what it is that some agent or agents must believe in virtue of which they can be said to accept that an act bears such-and-such a meaning. The argument so far has isolated two relevant types of belief, in the form of (I.1) and (I.25).

Some might want to insist that I have here two distinct types of meaning — but they would be mistaken; in both cases the meaning of an act is specified by giving its truth conditions, which relate the act, taken as performed in certain circumstances, to some state of affairs. The two cases differ, however, with respect to the types of belief which the agents have in virtue of which it can truly be said of them that they accept those meaning-relations as established.

I shall maintain that the second type of belief isolated, expressed in the form of (I.25), is the key to understanding what it is that creates the possibility of signalling and, indeed, of language use.

Griceans, I suppose, *would* want to say that I have here two types of meaning, and that somehow the basic ingredients of non-natural meaning have slipped into the account which led up to the introduction of (I.25). I think they are wrong if they claim that typically Gricean communicators' intentions are implicit in that account, although more needs to be said about the relationship between the grounds which a could have for taking an act of b to be non-deceiving, and a's beliefs about b's intentions in performing that act (see below, Sections III.5 and V.1). Against the Griceans, I want to say that they would have done well to look into the *similarities*, as well as the differences, between natural and non-natural meaning.

I do not intend that the discussion of (I.25) shall be taken to commit me to any conjectures about the way in which signalling systems actually come into being. My concern is with what creates the possibility of signalling and with what signalling is, and not with its origins/evolution. Granted that agents *can* have beliefs of the type attributed to *a* and *b* in (I.25), it matters not, for the concerns of this essay, how it comes about that agents do have such beliefs. It was convenient, for purposes of exposition, to lead up to (I.25) by imagining *a*'s situation when he realizes that an agent whose acts figure in his sign system becomes, potentially, a deceiver. But I do not believe for one minute that this is how all signalling systems actually develop.

Nor is the concern with the way in which an agent acquires knowledge of a signalling system; and, later on, nothing said will be taken as constituting an hypothesis about how people learn a language. I take it for granted that agents *can* learn the nature of rules of information, but *how* they do so is not my concern. If my claims are right, then we will know what sort of beliefs are acquired in the acquisition of a language: we will know part, at least, of what it is that learners have to learn.

Nor, finally, will I commit myself to any specific views about the grounds on which agents form and retain beliefs of type (I.25). It seems to me that various types of grounds should there be considered, if one were to try to decide on this matter, and that among those grounds consideration of communicators' intentions would be of importance; for example, it may well be that *a* and *b* form and retain a belief of type (I.25) because they believe they intend to try to provide a solution to some mutually recognized co-ordination problem. I have, of course, said something about the grounds on which agents might form and retain beliefs of type (I.1), and I have said that those grounds will be different from those behind beliefs of type (I.25) — and clearly they will be, for the latter type of belief concerns acts the performances of which are potentially deceiving, whereas the former does not.

Despite the disclaimer in the previous paragraph, let me repeat that I *am* concerned to consider the grounds on which an agent takes a particular performance of an act to be an instance of implementation of a rule of information. The relation between this question and the one raised in the previous paragraph is of some importance to the comparison I later make between aspects of my theory and Bennett's discussion of "intention-dependent" evidence.

The sorting out of these different questions may seem to be a very tedious business; but it is, I believe, an important task, the neglect of which has often given rise to confusions in the literature on the theories of meaning and use.

I.4. GENERALIZATION OF RULES OF INFORMATION

Signalling systems in which mutual beliefs of type (I.25) play a crucial role cannot be identified with Lewis indicative signalling systems; but there are sufficient important resemblances to justify using the term "signalling" in connection with both of them. However, before a detailed comparison can be made, some generalizations are required, for formula (I.25) pertains to one pair of agents and one type of action, tokens of which might be performed by one of them as signals to the other. A generalized form of (I.25) will eventually provide the basis of my account of what it is for a language to be a language of a population.

Let A be a set of act-types tokens of which can be performed by the individual members of a set C of agents. Let g be a function which assigns a type-specification to the acts performed by the members of C.

As before, let $Z, Z_1, Z_2, \ldots$ range over descriptions of particular situations or circumstances; these will be the circumstances in which acts of particular types are performed.

The function f_I will assign truth values to sentences at particular possible worlds; thus the domain of f_I will include pairs of the type (p, w), where w ranges over possible worlds. In addition, f_I will be given the role of assigning truth values to act-types: to all those act-types which are members of A, the act-types being specified in conjunction with a description of circumstances of performance, and the truth values being assigned by f_I at particular possible worlds.

These conditions of course allow it to be the case that not all acts of members of C are of a type which will be assigned a truth value, assuming that some of the acts performed by members of C are not instances of the act-types in A. They further grant that an act-type in A is assigned a truth value in a situation (a possible world) regardless of whether a token of that type is actually performed in that situation; but that surely does not matter (*cf*. Lewis, 1969, pp. 147–148). For example, the act-type described by "operating the right-hand side indicator of a car, whilst driving along the highway" is assigned the value true in any situation in which a driver on the highway is about to turn right (because that is what an act of that type means); with respect to any other situation it is assigned the value false. (Some may wish to insist that, in some possible worlds, an act-type should be assigned neither of the two truth values: for example in those possible worlds which lack the circumstances described by the Z factor included in the specification of the act-type. Thus, in possible worlds where there are no drivers and no highways, drivers' signals should perhaps be considered to be truthvalueless, rather than false. I have no objection to adopting such a move; it would amount to leaving the value of f_I undefined for at least those arguments whose possible world component lacks certain features, the presence of which is presupposed in the characterization of the act-type.)

An indicative signalling system (an ISS) may now be defined as a pair (A, f_I); this structure will be compared with a Lewis indicative signalling system (or LISS) in due course.

Where P is a set of agents (a population), an ISS will be said to be an ISS of P, or an ISS adopted by P, only if conditions (P1) and (P2) are both true for P and the ISS (A, f_I):

(P1)   The set C associated with the set A is such that $C \subseteq P$.

(P2)   For all p, for all q, for all Z, and for all pairs of individuals x, y (such that $x \in P$ and $y \in P$): if, for all w,
$f_I((g(E_x p), Z), w) = f_I(q, w)$ then
$B^*_{xy}((g(E_x p) \in A \cdot E_x p \cdot Z \cdot O_y(E_x p \cdot Z)) \to V_x q)$.

It is clear that the set C is thought of as the set of signallers. Note that (P1) requires subsetting, and not necessarily identity, between the set of signallers and the population; this is because there may be members of P who use the ISS but never in the role of communicator; perhaps they cannot perform the signalling acts, or perhaps they never have anything to communicate through the ISS; (cf. a similar point raised by Lewis in his revised account of conventions of truthfulness — see Lewis, 1975, p. 12).

(P2) is a development and generalization of (I.25). It says, essentially, that where x and y are both members of P and, for all possible worlds, x's doing p (in circumstances Z) has the same truth value as q, then x and y mutually believe that if x's doing p in Z is an instance of an act-type in A then x's doing p in Z means that q.

Are conditions (P1) and (P2) sufficient, as well as necessary, for the present task? I think not; their truth creates the possibility for the ISS to be a signalling system of P, or adopted by P, but it might still not be true that P's members have adopted the ISS — for they might still fail to relate performances of the signalling acts in A to their interest in being informed. If they *have* adopted the ISS they must surely be required to have some beliefs about standards which performances of the signalling acts ought, relative to that interest of theirs, to meet; they should be required to believe that it is optimal, relative to an audience's interest in being informed, that if a signal is given to that audience it is given non-deceivingly. I suggest, therefore, that (P3) needs to be added to (P1) and (P2):

(P3)   For all p, for all Z and for all pairs of individuals x, y (such that $x \in P$ and $y \in P$):
$$B_{xy}^* O_y((E_x p \cdot Z \cdot g(E_x p) \in A) \to O_y(E_x p \cdot Z)).$$

Perhaps the point behind (P3) might also be brought out as follows: it might have been the case that the members of P performed acts of the types included in A without being concerned about whether the performances were optimal relative to their interest in being informed; (P2) might still have held for them of course — they might well have been aware of what non-deceiving performances were signs of. But if this was the kind of attitude the members of P had to performances of acts of types included in A, then they could be said to exhibit a kind of *indifference* towards those performances, an indifference which — I suggest — would be incompatible with their having adopted (A, f_I) as a signalling system. When a population *does* adopt and use a signalling system the members need not, of course, believe that every act of signalling performed by a member is in fact optimal relative to their interest in being informed; but they must believe that *that* situation would itself be optimal, relative to that same interest; it is just this idea which (P3) is intended to capture.

I shall say, then, that an ISS is an ISS of, or adopted by, P if and only if (P1) and (P2) and (P3) all hold for that ISS and P.

These conditions focus on the mutual beliefs of individuals in the positions of signaller and audience, and ignore mutual beliefs which might be held among the members of audiences concerning acts of signalling which they together witness. I am following Lewis (revised version) in concentrating on the signaller-audience relationship; I shall not here develop the audience-audience dimension, but the tools are now available for that task.

I.5. ISS'S AND LEWIS INDICATIVE SIGNALLING SYSTEMS

Suppose that ISS is an indicative signalling system for a signalling problem *SP*. Suppose that LISS is a Lewis indicative signalling system for the same signalling problem. What differences, if any, are there between ISS and LISS?

In the original Lewis account LISS would be a pair (Fc, Fa), with Fa discretionary. The revised account has not been spelt out in full by Lewis in terms of the definition of the two functions, but presumably the idea is that Fc would remain as before — a function from states of affairs observed by the communicator to signalling actions. The domain of Fa would still be the set $\{o_k\}$ of signalling actions, but its range would now be a set of beliefs of a, or, granted that belief-formation or decision that such-and-such is the case can be taken to be an action, the range would be a set of actions of that sort. Presumably, under the revised account, the crucial point would still be that (Fc, Fa) is a LISS for SP if and only if $Fc/Fa = F$, but F would now describe the desired dependence in SP of audience *belief*, or *belief-formation*, on the state of affairs observed by c to hold.

Suppose that SP arises for c and a; behaviour in conformity with a LISS, (Fc, Fa), for SP would now look like this: if c observed s then he would give signal o if $Fc(s) = o$ (just as before, in the original version). And then a, observing o, would take the production of o as decisive grounds for believing that p, or for forming the belief that p, where $Fa(o) = B_a p$ or $Fa(o) = E_a B_a p$ (and $F(s) = B_a p$ or $F(s) = E_a B_a p$). So, if c and a conformed to the LISS they would be *truthful* and *trusting*, respectively.

In my definition of an ISS as a pair (A, f_I) there is no mention of what anyone believes or should believe − so this would appear to be a difference between an ISS and a LISS. But in Lewis (1969) there is an alternative mode offered for specifying a signalling system, which makes it look much more like an ISS and which can equally well be applied to the revised analysis of a LISS. According to this alternative mode, it is possible to specify a signalling system by means of a single function L, whose domain is the set of signalling actions $\{o_k\}$ of the system and whose range is a set of *interpretations*. An interpretation for Lewis is a pair (u, r); u is a mood indicator, showing whether a signal is indicative or imperative. Since the present concern is exclusively with indicative signals, this u component may be ignored. The r component is a truth condition and specifies, for each signalling action, the state of affairs in which it is true. Thus a LISS may be defined by giving $\{o_k\}$ and the truth condition of each member of $\{o_k\}$ − that is, as a pair, $(\{o_k\}, L)$, in which the first element is the counterpart of the set A in an ISS, and the second element is the counterpart of f_I in an ISS − with one difference, for my function assigns truth values to acts in situations or circumstances. But this remaining difference is not very significant, since such a modification could be incorporated within a LISS without altering its basic structure in any fundamental respect. An ISS is thus a slightly more elaborate specification of a LISS.

I have followed Lewis in assuming that his two modes of specifying a LISS are two descriptions of the same thing. It might be wondered whether this assumption is in fact correct; what happened to audience beliefs in the second specification? Are they just an inessential side-feature? The answer is that the second description is more abstract than the first in the sense that it abstracts from the communication situations in which the LISS will be used and concentrates on those features of the LISS in virtue of which its signals can be said to have meaning. The second specification presents the LISS as an abstract semantic system; the first shows how a pair of agents may use such a system to resolve a signalling problem.

As was already mentioned in Section I.1, Lewis himself has urged that a sharp distinction be drawn between the description of ". . . abstract semantic systems whereby symbols are associated with aspects of the world" and "the description of the psychological and sociological facts whereby a particular one of these abstract semantic systems is the one used by a person or population" (Lewis, 1972, p. 170). As I have said, I accept the distinction, but the substantial disagreement with Lewis concerns his specification of the conditions for adoption of such an abstract semantic system by a person or population.

Before discussing the details of that disagreement, it will be convenient to introduce a further development of a LISS, which can then be applied in modified form to an ISS.

Suppose that $(\{o_k\}, L)$ is a LISS whose $\{o_k\}$ consists of acts of *delivering* (that is, *uttering* or *writing*) verbal expressions. Following Lewis, a *verbal expression* is defined as "any finite sequence of types of vocal sounds or types of marks. To utter or to inscribe a verbal expression is to produce a string of sounds reverberating in the air or a string of marks on a surface". Furthermore, a *verbal signal* "is an action of uttering or inscribing a verbal expression" (Lewis, 1969, p. 142). If $\{o_k\}$ consists of verbal signals, then Lewis proposes the following modification: let the domain of L be not the signalling actions but the verbal expressions delivered in their performance. Then the domain of L is appropriately called the set of *sentences* of L and L itself is appropriately described as a *language*, the language associated with (Fc, Fa), (*op. cit.*, p. 152).

I want an account of a verbal indicative signalling system, a verbal ISS or VISS, to which my conditions (P2) and (P3) may be applied as they stand. So I prefer not to *replace* the set A of signalling actions by some set V of types of verbal expressions. Instead, I propose the following moves: a VISS will be defined as a quintuple $(A, V, f_v^1, f_v^2, f_I)$ in which the elements A and f_I remain defined as they were for an ISS. V is the set of types of verbal expressions in the VISS. For any pair $(E_a p, Z)$ such that $g(E_a p) \in A$, f_v^1 assigns a pair (v, Z), where $v \in V$. Intuitively, f_v^1 assigns to each type of signalling act in A a type of verbal expression – the one delivered in a performance of a token of a signalling act of that type. The context or circumstance factor, which accompanies the specification of types of signalling acts, also accompanies the specification of the types of verbal expression associated with them. The reason for "carrying over" the indicator of context in this way is obvious: indication of context is required not only in specifying truth conditions for signalling acts, but also in giving the truth conditions for the verbal expressions.

The function f_v^2 assigns truth values at possible worlds to each element in the range of f_v^1. Thus f_v^2, like f_I, is a function which determines truth conditions, whereas f_v^1 shows which verbal expression-type is exhibited by each verbal signalling act-type. The specification of a VISS is completed by requiring that the truth condition assigned by f_I to a verbal signalling act-type will be identical to the truth condition assigned by f_v^2 to the verbal expression-type which that verbal signalling act-type exhibits.

That I do not make a distinction between the meaning of a verbal signalling act-type and the meaning of its associated type of verbal expression seems to me to be quite in order, given that I *do* draw the distinction (as mentioned earlier) between meaning in the sense now under discussion and the notion of what a speaker means by (intends to do by) saying what he says. This latter notion pertains to an agent's intentions in performing a signalling act and thus, unlike the former notion, is appropriately analysed in terms of the modality Shall.

It is now possible to define what it is for a VISS to be adopted by a population: a VISS $(A, V, f_v^1, f_v^2, f_I)$ is a VISS of population P, or a VISS adopted by P, if and only if (P1), (P2) and (P3) are all true for the VISS and P.

The definition, like the earlier one for ISS adoption, should not be taken to imply that the members of P are all set-theorists, any more than a physiologist's account of something people regularly do (like breathing) implies that we are all physiologists. Of course the members of P will most likely not describe the elements of A and V, in a VISS they have adopted, in the way I have described them (*cf.* Lewis, 1975, pp. 24–5).

It seems to me that it is quite right that the structure of the generalized rule of information (P2) should remain essentially unchanged when the "progression" is made to verbal signalling; why should *that* change just because the signallers are now making noises or inscriptions rather than, e.g., hanging lanterns or giving some kind of manual signals?

When (P2) and (P3) are applied to a case in which the VISS concerned is a natural language, some weakening in the conditions will be required, for the simple reason that some members of P will know more about the language than others. How much familiarity with the language must be common among the members of P? It is impossible to determine – I think we just have to require, for a minimal set of conditions for language adoption by P, that (P2) and (P3) must hold for a minimal subset of A (and thus for a minimal subset of V), a subset sufficiently large to justify the claim that the members of P are competent in the language. In that way the account of language adoption could allow that some members of P are more articulate than others. But no fundamental change in the structure of (P2) would be called for; if a problem arises here (and I think it does not), it would also I believe arise within Lewis's account.

Lewis goes on towards a fuller specification of what a *natural language* is, in Chapter V of his 1969 book and in his 1975 paper. He there indicates the differences between the structure of a (verbal) LISS, considered as an abstract semantic system, and that of a natural language (English), also considered as an abstract semantic system. And the formal structure of English is developed in greater detail by him in his 1972 paper, along lines comparable to those taken by others also working in the tradition of model-theoretic semantics.

It seems to me that the structure of a verbal LISS, or of a VISS, can be enriched in such a way as to come closer and closer to providing a formal model of a natural language (without non-declaratives), without thereby necessitating any fundamental change in the account of what it is for a language to be the language adopted by some population P. And on this point I believe I am following the basic strategy in Lewis's work.

It has already been mentioned that a VISS is in one respect a richer structure than a verbal LISS, because it contains the context indicator, the Z factor. In that respect a VISS already corresponds more closely to a formal model of a natural language than does a verbal LISS. The *further* elaboration required may be summed up by saying that, to provide a model for a natural language, a much more detailed specification is needed of the input to the function called f_v^2. The first elements of the input comprise pairs, the first terms of which are types of verbal expressions and the second terms of which are indicators of context. Clearly, in order to describe a natural language the class of verbal expressions *of* that language must be defined – that is, a *grammar* is needed; and it must be decided which sorts of contextual or circumstantial factors are relevant to the determination of meanings.

This two-fold task is Lewis's main concern in his paper "General Semantics". He there describes a categorially-based transformational grammar which, as any adequate grammar must, aims to define the class of well-formed verbal expressions (sentences) of the language, and assigns to each sentence a structural description. Among other things, the theory developed shows how to accommodate the phenomena of *word-meaning* and *phrase-meaning*, as well as sentence-meaning; and it provides an explanation of how ambiguities can arise because of structure — because of the fact that sentences are (usually) composite or compound. For example, how else could the ambiguity of "The Eighth Army push bottles up the Germans" be explained except by reference to structural description? Also, Lewis describes various other kinds of factors which have to be included in the specification of the input to those functions which determine truth conditions for (structurally described) sentences. Among the factors needed are: a time coordinate, a place co-ordinate, a speaker coordinate, an audience coordinate, an indicated object coordinate (to cope, for example, with demonstrative pronouns and demonstrative adjectives), and a previous discourse coordinate. In terms of my own account of a VISS, I think that these coordinates could be introduced as an extensive elaboration of the Z factor which describes features of context of delivery of a verbal expression and which, in virtue of f_v^1, is also assigned to the verbal expression itself.

Thus the verbal expressions require structural description assigned by a grammar; and the specification of context requires elaboration in the way just indicated. It is beyond the scope of this essay to go into further detail on this issue. The point is merely to *suggest* how the enrichment of the structure of a VISS *might* proceed, so as to provide a formal model of a natural language; an essential aim of the essay is to provide a framework for the account of language *use* within which the approach of the formal semanticists to the analysis of linguistic structure may be incorporated. But the details of the formal semanticists' proposals are not my immediate concern.

(It may be asked whether the fact that reference will be made to speakers' intentions, in such coordinates as the indicated objects coordinate, provides any support to the Gricean theory. The question should be answered in the negative: the fact that some sentences in the language (e.g., those containing demonstratives) require reference to be made to utterer's intentions in the specification of their truth conditions does *not* justify the claim that the concept of utterer's intention is logically primitive in the analysis of what meaning *is* — any more than the fact that we also have coordinates for time and place (among others) implies that the concept of meaning must itself be analysed in terms of the concepts of time and place. A further consideration here is that it will be *in virtue of* his knowledge of what the sentences delivered to him *mean* that a hearer is able to decide which, if any, of the speaker's intentions are relevant to the determination of the truth values which those sentences actually have.)

The question which now remains is this: how does my account of language adoption differ from Lewis's?

I.6. CONVENTIONS OF TRUTHFULNESS AND TRUST V RULES OF INFORMATION

"*L* is an *actual language* of *P* if and only if there prevails in *P* a convention of truthfulness in *L*, sustained by an interest in communication" (Lewis, 1969, p. 194).

This was Lewis's earlier definition of what it is for a possible language *L* to be an actual language of a population *P*. According to that earlier account, the conventions relevant to a description of language use were based not on speaker-hearer coordination but on "... the diffuse coordination between the present speaker and the past speakers who trained the present hearer" (Lewis, 1975, p. 11). No conformative behaviour on the part of the *hearer* was called for, in the earlier account, because Lewis considered only co-ordination between *actions*, and "the proper hearer's response to consider is believing" (*loc. cit.*).

As indicated in Section I.1 above, Lewis's *revised* account incorporates "the proper hearer's response" and, consequently, if *c* and *a* conform to a LISS they are truthful and trusting, respectively. (*Fc, Fa*) would be a conventional LISS (for a signalling problem *SP*) if *c* and *a* regularly conformed to (*Fc, Fa*) in their respective ways, when confronted by *SP*. From this basis, the generalised account of language use or adoption by a population takes the following form: "A language *L* is *used by* a population *P* if and only if there prevails in *P* a convention of truthfulness and trust in *L*, sustained by an interest in communication" (Lewis, 1975, p. 10).

I do not dispute that the revised account constitutes an improvement on the earlier version; but I claim that both are wrong, and for the same reason. If *P* exhibits a convention of truthfulness and trust in *L* sustained by an interest in communication, then that is sufficient to guarantee that *P* adopts *L*. But I dispute the *necessity* of a convention of truthfulness, and of a convention of truthfulness and trust. I do not propose to register dis-agreement with Lewis's definition of convention. But given that a convention is a regularity R, in action or in action and belief, in a population P, such that, with a "few exceptions to the "everyone's"" tolerated:

(1)   Everyone conforms to R.
(2)   Everyone believes that the others conform to R (Lewis, 1975, p. 5)

then I think that Lewis has confused that which *preserves* a practice with that which *constitutes* it.

I have no doubt that, as a matter of fact, truthfulness and trust is generally widespread among the members of a language-using population, and that it is generally widespread because of an interest in communication; regular conformity of the type Lewis requires of language-users preserves the language as a means of meeting such an interest. But regular conformity of this sort is *more* than enough to create the possibility of indicative language use in P. What is essential is that the members of P are mutually aware of what *would* be true if, when a well-informed communicator delivers some verbal expression in their language, they could be confident that he was trustworthy. What speaker and hearer must be mutually aware of is what non-deceiving performance by the speaker would be evidence of for the hearer; it is a contingent and not necessary feature of language use that speakers and hearers are frequently truthful and trusting, respectively.

So condition (P2) is the key part of my alternative to Lewis's convention of truthfulness and trust. If (P2) were false for P and some language L then some, at least, of the members of P would fail to be mutually aware of the significance of some act or acts of delivering an expression in L. For some such act or acts they would be unaware of what its (their) trustworthy performance would be evidence of or a sign of. It was granted that (P2) should not be required to hold for all linguistic acts whose type is in A, but that it must hold for a large enough subset of them to justify the claim that P's members are competent in the language. But if, relative to that subset, (P2) fails, then that language is not a language of P (although it might still be a language of some subset of P).

Of course instances of communication situations which do not exhibit truthfulness and trust are by no means uncommon. Imagine b communicates with a: a does not trust b and is perhaps justified in taking this attitude on this occasion and many others; but a is still aware of the meaning of b's communicative act; for he is aware of what would be true if b's act could be trusted. He is aware also, perhaps, of what b's purpose might be in performing that act; it is not clear to me how Lewis's account is able to cope with this kind of situation, although mine can.

According to Lewis, the convention of truthfulness and trust is sustained by an interest in communication among the members of P. In Lewis, 1969, p. 181, an interest in communication is described as an interest "... in being able to control one another's beliefs and actions, to some extent, by means of sounds and marks". This description seems to be too speaker-biased for his revised account, which returns to speaker-hearer coordination (See Lewis, 1975). There, for indicative communication, it would seem that an interest in communication will amount to an interest in receiving information and in being able to influence one another's beliefs. My condition (P3) was designed to guarantee that the members of P relate the ISS, VISS or natural language to their interest, *qua* audience, in being reliably informed, and I have assumed that they have such an interest. I have no objection to adding the further requirement that, *qua* communicators, they have an interest in influencing one another's beliefs. Given that they are users of the communication system, my conditions put them in the position in which they can try to meet that interest.

Suppose that L is a language of P and that b, a member of P, delivers a sentence of L which means that q. Then, on Lewis's account, unless b's act is one of the very few exceptions which can be tolerated, b intends to be truthful, and he intends that his audience a shall trust him: he intends to produce in a the belief that q. Thus it is central to Lewis's account that when b uses L part of the Gricean conditions for non-natural meaning, at least as they were originally formulated, must be satisfied. But my account of language use is "Grice-free", in the sense that a communicator may perform his communicative act without having any of the specifically Gricean intentions; (the question of what intentions he must have is discussed further in Chapters III and V).

I do not deny that the central use of indicative language is that of showing how things stand: the reliable transmission of reliable information. Lewis's account and mine accept this fact, but we employ it in different ways. My aim is to try to provide an account of indicative language use which takes the afore-mentioned central function of such language as a focal point, yet which remains sufficiently independent of it to provide a basis for the analysis of other uses of such language as well. For example, according to Lewis's theory, cases of dishonesty, deceit and lack of trust in L have got to be exceptional – they have to be seen as *abuse* of language. It seems to me, however, that deceit in L is something which occurs quite regularly and that it should be viewed as a commonplace feature of the use of language. My account will allow language-users to be a good deal more devious, and suspicious, whereas Lewis's language-users are required to be saints with Gricean intentions.

In the dialogue of "objections" and "replies" in his 1975 paper, Lewis raises two objections relevant to the present point: how does his approach explain the possibility of the following sorts of usage of language: irony, metaphor, joking, telling tall tales, telling white lies, and so on? (Lewis, 1975, pp. 28–29). His replies, I think, bring out the inflexibility of his theory, for he resorts to the expedient of creating sub-languages of, and extensions of, the language L. Thus, if the members of P use irony and metaphor then Lewis allows that they are truthful in L (their language), but not *literally* truthful, and he continues: "To be literally truthful in L is to be truthful in another language related to L, a language we can call literal-L. The relation between L and literal-L is as follows: a good way to describe L is to start by specifying literal-L and then to describe L as obtained by certain systematic departures from literal-L" (*op. cit.*, p. 28). Similarly, in any cases of language-use in which members of P are joking or telling tall tales or white lies, then: ". . . their seeming untruthfulness in non-serious situations is untruthfulness not in the language L that they actually use, but only in a simplified approximation to L" (*loc. cit.*). So the strategy seems to be to mark out sub-sections or extensions of L for each type of "non-standard" usage of L — so that, in the end, it can be denied that there are any non-standard usages of L at all . . . they are, rather, usages of something L-like.

Maybe the details of such a procedure can be worked out, but it seems to me to be uneconomical and misguided; for it gives no clear picture of how it is that *one* language can be exploited for various purposes. In Chapter III I give some examples of how to analyse some types of non-standard usage of indicative language; the basic hypothesis will be that such uses trade on, and are made possible by, mutual beliefs of the type employed in the characterization of rules of information. Even in cases of irony, some types of jokes, metaphor, in which the speaker may make it perfectly clear to his audience (by means of gesture, facial expression, or other features of the style of presentation of the linguistic act) that he is *not* being literally truthful, there is often reliance on mutual beliefs about what *would* have had to have been the case if the speaker's utterance *had* been literally truthful. The speaker may often rely on such beliefs in order to achieve an intended effect.

It should be pointed out that Lewis does suggest an alternative possible approach to the problems created by non-standard usage. This alternative, as he says, would require a modification in his overall theory. It involves changing the definition of what it is for L to be a language of P, so that L becomes a language of P on the weaker condition that there prevails in P a convention of truthfulness and trust in L *in serious communication situations* (Lewis, 1975, p. 29). "If that much is a convention in P, it does not matter what goes on in other situations: they use L." As Lewis himself observes, the definition he gives of "serious communication situation" resembles closely the definition of a *signalling problem* in Chapter IV of his 1969 book. Now Lewis proved in Section 5 of that chapter that if c gives a signal in conformity with a conventional signalling system then his act has Gricean non-natural meaning. So speakers in P use L, on this new definition, only if their speech acts are accompanied by the *full range* of Gricean intentions. But how can Lewis dismiss so readily "what goes on in other situations", which are not fully Gricean? The possibility of *various* uses of indicative language is something which the theory of language use needs to explain.

Given that Lewis's original set of conditions for language adoption is sufficient, they must entail mine, if mine are correct; and so they do: it is obvious that (P1) is entailed; Lewis language-users are truthful and trusting, so they are aware of what they have to do to be truthful and trusting — so (P2) holds for them; (P3) holds for them because they have an interest in communication.

Finally, note that Lewis's approach to these questions is inspired by Stenius's penetrating but (sadly) neglected paper "Mood and Language-Game" (Stenius, 1967). (It seems incredible that Stenius's paper has received so little attention from speech-act theorists.) In a revealing footnote, Lewis says the following about Stenius (quotation in full here serves the purpose also of introducing the basic features, in barest outline, of Stenius's theory): "He proposes that language use is governed by rules giving truth conditions for sentence-radicals (sentences minus their indicators of mood) and by rules prescribing the appropriate sort of truthfulness for each mood. He considers three moods: indicatives, imperatives and yes-no interrogatives. I have adopted his proposal by building truth conditions into the identification of possible languages and by taking his rules of truthfulness as conventions of truthfulness . . ." (Lewis, 1969, p. 177, fn. 8).

Stenius's main concern in his paper is to characterise the semantic rules governing the indicative, imperative and interrogative modal elements. His rule for the indicative mood is as follows (it corresponds with Lewis's convention of truthfulness):

"Produce a sentence in the indicative mood only if its sentence-radical is true" (*op. cit.*, p. 268). And he says concerning this rule that it is "... a rule for the 'speaker' — the person who makes the linguistic move — and it says under what conditions such a move is correct" (*loc. cit.*). He goes to some lengths in explaining in what sense of "semantic" his rule *is* a semantic rule. If a speaker violates the rule he may still nevertheless be making a move in the indicative language-game (p. 269). The rule is not like a rule of chess, for example; if one's move breaks a rule of chess one has failed to make a chess-move at all.

In some interesting comments on Stenius's paper, Føllesdal has concentrated on the question of what kind of rule Stenius's rules are (Føllesdal, 1967). He mentions the example used by von Neumann and Morgenstern, who distinguish between forbidden "moves" and unwise moves in chess. One cannot make a chess "move" placing one's king in check — it is forbidden. But one can of course move into a position which is such that the opponent wins checkmate at his next move — that is not forbidden, but just unwise (in this case losing) strategy.

Føllesdal maintains, perhaps with justification, that Stenius's rules are a kind of strategic rule "... which ought to be followed if the language-game is to keep its character as a *language-game* i.e., a game of communication. They may be broken without the game coming to an end, but if they are broken frequently, the communicational character of the language-game will be impaired. We could call them *preservative* rules, as distinguished from the rules of the game properly so called, which for clarity we might call *constitutive* rules" (*op. cit.*, p. 279). While I think that the notion of *communication* implied by Føllesdal's remarks is too narrow, his basic distinction is interesting, and earlier in this section I used it in criticizing Lewis. For Lewis's convention of truthfulness and trust is preservative of indicative language use, not constitutive of it, and yet it is clear that he takes himself to be providing an account of what it *is* for a language to be a language of a population.

I am not entirely certain about Føllesdal's classification of Stenius's rules, for it seems that some of what Stenius has to say concerning them suggests a close similarity with my (P3); my earlier account gives to (P3) a more than merely preservative function.

Whatever might be said about similarities between Stenius's rules and mine, there are considerable *differences* between his rules and Lewis's conventions: where Stenius talks of what ought to be, or shall be, done (he does not distinguish these), Lewis talks of regularities in behaviour − of what will be done. Thus the modalities involved in their respective characterizations of linguistic rules are quite different.

I admit that if conventions of truthfulness and trust were violated frequently, then language *learning* would become difficult, if not impossible; and perhaps certain patterns of violation of trust in communication may play a role in the development of schizophrenic behaviour (*cf.*, below, Chapter VI). Føllesdal indeed suggests that rules which may be merely preservative of language *use* are in fact constitutive of language *learning*. (For some further comments on Stenius, see Jones, 1981.)

CHAPTER II

A FORMAL LANGUAGE

II.1. LC: ITS SYNTAX AND THE GENERAL FORM
OF ITS SEMANTICS

Some illustrations of the expressive powers of LC were given in Chapter I. The purpose of the formal language is to permit precise description of various types of interpersonal interaction, including those which are centrally involved in communication. The next task is to define that language, and to discuss some of its main properties.

Since LC is intended to serve the purpose just indicated, it must be capable of being used to describe an agent's knowledge of his own language(s), signalling system(s) and sign system(s). Elementary set theory was already employed, in the first chapter, to describe the content of this knowledge. So it will be assumed from the outset that LC contains the language of elementary set theory. Thus, any well-formed formula of elementary set theory is a wff of LC.

LC is a pair (V, Q), where V is the set of wffs of LC and Q is a function which assigns to each member of V its truth conditions.

The members of V are constructed in certain ways from elements contained in the following sets of symbols:

VP: a set of predicate letters.
VX: a set of individual constants and individual variables.
VM: a set of symbols for modalities.
VT: a set of truth-functional operators.
VB: a set of punctuation symbols – parentheses.
VQu: a set of quantifiers.

A subset of VX, called VC, contains all those individual constants in VX which name individuals which can be said to have knowledge, to have beliefs and to perform acts. And VC contains variables ranging over such individuals. We thus refer to VC as the set of agent individual constants and agent individual variables.

If a is an individual variable or constant symbol and $O \in$ VM and O is *relativized to a*, then we write $O_a \in$ VM.

41

VT contains the following:

$\sim$, the negation sign.
$\rightarrow$, the material implication sign.
$\vee$, the disjunction sign.
$\cdot$, the conjunction sign.
$\leftrightarrow$, the material equivalence sign.

The set VQu contains the symbols (x) and $(\exists x)$, in which x is any individual variable symbol; these symbols are called the universal and existential quantifier, respectively.

Any finite sequence of symbols is a well-formed formula of LC if and only if it is of one of the following forms (*cf.* Pörn, 1977, Chapter 1):

1. $N(a_1, a_2, \ldots, a_k)$ where the k-place predicate letter N is a member of VP and each member of the sequence $(a_1, a_2, \ldots, a_k)$ is either an individual constant or individual variable symbol;
2. $\sim p$, $(p \cdot q)$, $(p \vee q)$, $(p \rightarrow q)$, or $(p \leftrightarrow q)$ where p and q are wffs of LC;
3. Op where p is a wff of LC and $O \in$ VM (relativized or unrelativized).
4. $(x)p$ or $(\exists x)p$ where p is a wff of LC and x is an individual variable symbol occurring in p.
5. All well-formed sequences of symbols of elementary set theory are wffs of LC.

This completes the definition of the set V, the set of wffs of LC.

It is next shown how the function Q assigns truth-conditions to the members of V, beginning with the definition of the symbols in VT.

Let the letters T and F designate the truth values *true* and *false*, respectively.

W is the set of possible worlds; Q assigns truth values to members of V in members of W. An expression of the form $Q(p, w) = T$ should be read as: "Q assigns the value T to p in w" or "p is true in w", where w is a member of W.

Let p and q be any members of V and let w be any member of W; then the following conditions hold:

(Q$\sim$) $Q(\sim p, w) = T$ iff $Q(p, w) \neq T$
(QF) $Q(p, w) = F$ iff $Q(\sim p, w) = T$
(Q$\sim\sim$) $Q(\sim\sim p, w) = T$ iff $Q(p, w) = T$

(Q∨) $Q((p \lor q), w) = T$ iff either $Q(p, w) = T$ or
$Q(q, w) = T$

(Q·) $Q((p \cdot q), w) = T$ iff $Q(p, w) = T$ and $Q(q, w) = T$

(Q→) $Q((p \to q), w) = T$ iff either $Q(\sim p, w) = T$ or
$Q(q, w) = T$

(Q↔) $Q((p \leftrightarrow q), w) = T$ iff either $Q(p, w) = T$ and
$Q(q, w) = T$ or $Q(p, w) = F$ and $Q(q, w) = F$

Let the function Q^+ assign to each $w \in W$ a non-empty set of individuals: the individuals which exist in w.

Let Q^- be a function which assigns to each member of VP, for each world in W, its extension in that world. That is, where $N \in$ VP is a k-place predicate, $Q^-(N, w)$ is a set, possibly empty, of ordered k-tuples of individuals in w. It is assumed that, where N is a k-place predicate, $Q^-(N, w) \subseteq (Q^+(w))^k$, where $(Q^+(w))^k$ denotes the set of all ordered k-tuples of individuals existing in w. Then the following condition holds:

(QN) Where $(a_1, a_2, \ldots, a_k)$ is any sequence of k individual constant symbols, $Q(N(a_1, a_2, \ldots, a_k), w) = T$ iff the ordered sequence of individuals designated by $(a_1, a_2, \ldots, a_k)$ is a member of $Q^-(N, w)$.

Again, let w be any member of W; let p be any member of V containing at least one occurrence of the individual variable symbol x; let $p(a/x)$ denote the result of replacing each occurrence of x in p by one of the individual constant symbol a. Assume further that each member of $Q^+(w)$ is assigned an individual constant symbol. Then the following conditions hold:

(QU) $Q((x)p, w) = T$ iff $Q(p(a/x), w) = T$ for each individual constant symbol a which denotes a member of $Q^+(w)$.

(Q∃) $Q((\exists x)p, w) = T$ iff $Q(p(a/x), w) = T$ for at least one individual constant symbol a which denotes a member of $Q^+(w)$.

In formulating truth conditions for modalized formulae in V, it is convenient first to give a list of generalized conditions; with the exception of the modalities B_a and V_a, the particular modalities in LC (discussed each in turn below) can be defined in terms of appropriate subsets of these generalized conditions. Since only one of these modalities is not relativized, the generalized conditions are stated for relativized operators; the simple changes needed for the conditions for the unrelativized operators will be specified below, in the presentation of the modality concerned.

With each $O_a \in$ VM, where a is an individual variable or constant symbol in VC, we associate a binary relation $R(O_a)$, called an accessibility relation. Such a relation is defined over a set of possible worlds — it is a relation of accessibility between possible worlds.

In what follows let w, w_1, w_2 be any members of W, and let O_a be any relativized member of VM:

(QM1) $Q(O_a p, w) = $ T iff $Q(p, w_1) = $ T for all w_1 such that (w, w_1) $\in R(O_a)$, where a denotes any agent individual in $Q^+(w)$.

(QM2) $Q(\sim O_a \sim p, w) = $ T iff $Q(p, w_1) = $ T for at least one w_1 such that $(w, w_1) \in R(O_a)$, where a denotes any agent individual in $Q^+(w)$.

(QM3) $Q(O_a p, w) = $ T iff $Q(p, w_1) = $ F for all w_1 such that (w, w_1) $\in R(O_a)$, where a denotes any agent individual in $Q^+(w)$.

(QM4) $Q(\sim O_a \sim p, w) = $ T iff $Q(p, w_1) = $ F for at least one w_1 such that $(w, w_1) \in R(O_a)$, where a denotes any agent individual in $Q^+(w)$.

(Q.Ser) $R(O_a)$ is serial; i.e., for each $w \in$ W there is some $w_1 \in$ W such that $(w, w_1) \in R(O_a)$.

(Q.Ref) $R(O_a)$ is reflexive; i.e., for each $w \in$ W, $(w, w) \in R(O_a)$.

(Q. Trans) $R(O_a)$ is transitive; i.e., for all w, w_1, $w_2 \in$ W, if (w, w_1) $\in R(O_a)$ and $(w_1, w_2) \in R(O_a)$ then $(w, w_2) \in R(O_a)$.

(Q.Euclid) $R(O_a)$ is euclidean; i.e., for all w, w_1, $w_2 \in$ W, if (w, w_1) $\in R(O_a)$ and $(w, w_2) \in R(O_a)$ then $(w_1, w_2) \in R(O_a)$.

A wff p of LC is said to be contradictory in LC iff there is no world $w \in$ W such that $Q(p, w) = $ T. A wff p of LC is said to be valid in LC, or a theorem of LC, iff $\sim p$ is contradictory in LC.

Suppose that q is a wff of LC; and suppose that $\{p_1, p_2, \ldots, p_n\}$ is a finite set of wffs of LC; then q will be said to be a logical consequence in LC of $\{p_1, p_2, \ldots, p_n\}$ iff the wff $((p_1 \cdot p_2 \cdot \ldots \cdot p_n) \rightarrow q)$ is a theorem of LC.

When it is said, of any wff of LC, that it is provable, I shall mean by that that the wff can be shown to be valid.

My usage of the metalogical terminology departs to some extent from standard practice, but this will be quite harmless in the context of the present essay.

II.2. ACTION MODALITIES

If we adopt from the set of truth conditions for modalized sentences the conditions (QM1), (QM2), and (Q.Ref), replacing in them each occurrence of O_a by one of D_a, and then replacing $\sim D_a\sim$ in (QM2) by C_a, then we have the logic of action from Pörn (1970), for which sentences of the form $D_a p$ were read: "*a* brings it about that *p*" and those of the form $C_a p$ were read: "it is possible for all that *a* does that *p*". The shortcomings of this logic for act-descriptions have been discussed elsewhere (e.g., Pörn, 1970, 1974, 1977; and Jones, 1970); as a (relativised) semantical analogue of the alethic modal system T it of course validates the rule (R1):

(R1) If *p* is a theorem then $D_a p$ is a theorem.

And it contains (II.1) as a theorem:

(II.1) $(D_a p \cdot D_a(p \rightarrow q)) \rightarrow D_a q$

from which it immediately follows that, for any theorem of the form $(p \rightarrow q)$, if it is true that *a* brings it about that *p* then it is true that *a* brings it about that *q*. Thus in this logic it is provably the case that any agent brings about all logical truths and, furthermore, that any agent brings about all the logical consequences of what he does.

A striking illustration of the unacceptability of this second feature is provided by the attempt to combine this logic of action with a logic of knowledge, so that formulae of the following form — which are by no means irrelevant to the description of interpersonal communication — may be constructed:

(II.2) $D_a K_b p$.

Given that any logic containing a logic of knowledge must validate (II.3): $K_b p \rightarrow p$, then (R1) will validate (II.4) $D_a(K_b p \rightarrow p)$, and hence (II.2) will logically imply (II.5): $D_a p$. So it is provably the case in such a logic that if *a* brings it about that *b* knows that *p* then *a* brings it about that *p*.

A solution to these problems has been provided in Kanger (1972) and Pörn (1974). It rests on an appreciation of why it is absurd to suppose that an agent brings about a logical truth. Genuine agency on the part of *a* requires that things *might* (at least) not have been as they are had *a* not acted in the way he did. Logical truths are beyond the scope of anyone's *agency*. The solution requires adoption of (QM3) and (QM4), replacing each occurrence in them of O_a by one of D'_a, and then rewriting $\sim D'_a \sim$ in (QM4) as C'_a. The operators may be given the following readings (*cf.*, Pörn, 1977, pp. 5–7):

$D'_a p$:   "but for a's action it would not be the case that p";
$C'_a p$:   "but for a's action it might not be the case that p".

The accessibility relation $R(D'_a)$ is to be understood in the following way: imagine that a fails to perform one or more of the actions which he does in fact perform at w; what will w now be like? It may surely be supposed that various outcomes are possible, and where $(w, w_1) \in R(D'_a)$ it is understood that w_1 represents one such outcome. The set of *all* w_1 such that $(w, w_1) \in R(D'_a)$ will thus represent the set of all those outcomes which might be realized if a fails to perform one or more of the actions which he does in fact perform at w. If $\sim p$ is true in every such outcome, then it must be true of w that, but for a's action, it *would* not be the case that p. If $\sim p$ is true of at least one such outcome, then it must be true of w that, but for a's action, it *might* not be the case that p.

This way of characterizing the relation $R(D'_a)$ differs from that suggested by Pörn (*op. cit.*, p. 5), who requires, for each w_1 such that $(w, w_1) \in R(D'_a)$, that the opposite of *everything* a does at w is the case at w_1; it seems to me that *this* way of interpreting the relation commits Pörn to Kanger's analysis of the action logic (see below), an analysis which he in fact wishes to reject.

Given the intuitive interpretation of the relation $R(D'_a)$, it is clear that it must be assumed to be irreflexive. Furthermore, it is reasonable to adopt (Q.Ser) for this relation, with the immediate consequence that (II.6) is a theorem: (II.6) $D'_a p \rightarrow C'_a p$. Further properties of $R(D'_a)$ will be discussed in due course.

It is clear that sentences of the form $D_a p$ are not properly read as "a brings it about that p"; I follow Pörn and Kanger in adopting the reading "p is necessary for something that a does" (i.e., "$\sim p$ is incompatible with something a does"). Thus it is right to suppose that $D_a p$ captures *part* of the meaning of "a brings it about that p" — for it is obvious that if a brings it about that p then p is necessary for something that a does. But the converse fails; for the truth of "a brings it about that p" it is required not merely that p is necessary for something a does but *also* that, but for a's action, it might not be the case that p. So I adopt Pörn's proposal that formulae of the form $E_a p$ (read as "a brings it about that p") be defined as follows:

(Df.E) $E_a p =_{df} (D_a p \cdot C'_a p)$.

An alternative definition, call it (Df.E1), has been proposed by Kanger (*op. cit.*):

(Df.E1) $E_a p =_{df} (D_a p \cdot D'_a p)$.

This definition seems plainly counter-intuitive, for it is quite conceivable that *a* brings about *p* and that *p might* still have been the case even if he had not acted in the way that he did; but I have an alternative way of demonstrating the inadequacy of (Df.E1): suppose that

(i) $Q(E_a p, w) = T$
and (ii) $Q(E_a (p \rightarrow q), w) = T$

for some $w \in W$, and suppose further that (Df.E1) is adopted. Then:

from (i), (iii) $Q((D_a p \cdot D'_a p), w) = T$
" (ii), (iv) $Q((D_a (p \rightarrow q) \cdot D'_a (p \rightarrow q)), w) = T$
" (iii), (v) $Q(D'_a p, w) = T$, by (Q·)
" (iv), (vi) $Q(D'_a (p \rightarrow q), w) = T$, by (Q·).

But $R(D'_a)$ is serial; i.e., for some $w_1 \in W, (w, w_1) \in R(D'_a)$.

Thus, from (v), (vii) $Q(p, w_1) = F$, by (QM3)
and from (vi), (viii) $Q((p \rightarrow q), w_1) = F$, by (QM3). Hence,
from   (viii), (ix) $Q(p, w_1) = T$ $\Big]$ By (Q→), (Q~),
    and (x) $Q(q, w_1) = F$ $\Big]$ (Q F) and (Q~~).

By (Q F), lines (vii) and (ix) violate (Q~). So the proof shows that, according to (Df.E1), it is contradictory to suppose that any agent *a* brings it about that *p* and brings it about that if *p* then *q*. This appears to be conclusive grounds for preferring (Df.E) to (Df.E1), since the contradiction demonstrated cannot be derived if D'_a is replaced by C'_a. The condition (QM4), appropriate for the evaluation of sentences of type $C'_a p$, does *not* require the falsity of *p* and the falsity of $(p \rightarrow q)$ in the same world.

So I adopt (Df.E). What further properties, if any, should be added to the relations $R(D_a)$ and $R(D'_a)$? Note that (II.7) and (II.8), below, are theorems, in virtue (essentially) of the reflexivity of $R(D_a)$:

(II.7) $E_a p \rightarrow p$
(II.8) $E_a E_a p \rightarrow E_a p$.

But what about the converse of (II.8)? If it was a theorem, then of course formulae of forms $E_a p$ and $E_a E_a p$ would be provably equivalent. I see no good reason for denying this equivalence, but, as our conditions stand, (II.9) is not a theorem:

(II.9) $E_a p \rightarrow E_a E_a p$.

So the conditions need to be strengthened in various ways. To see *which* ways, consider that the consequent of (II.9) is, by (Df.E), equivalent to the conjunction: $(D_a(D_a p \cdot C'_a p) \cdot C'_a E_a p)$. By the logic as it stands we have:

(II.10) $C'_a p \rightarrow C'_a E_a p$

hence $C'_a E_a p$ is implied by $E_a p$. By the logic of the D_a operator, the wff $D_a(D_a p \cdot C'_a p)$ is equivalent to $(D_a D_a p \cdot D_a C'_a p)$. We now add to the conditions the requirement (Q.Trans) applied to $R(D_a)$. Thus

(II.11) $D_a p \rightarrow D_a D_a p$

is a theorem, and so $E_a p$ implies $D_a D_a p$. So there remains the problem how

(II.12) $E_a p \rightarrow D_a C'_a p$

is to be validated in LC. Given what has already been said about the logic of action it is clear that $D_a p$ cannot be allowed to imply $D_a C'_a p$. However,

(II.13) $C'_a p \rightarrow D_a C'_a p$

is entirely acceptable. To see this more clearly, consider the alternative readings for $D'_a p$ and $C'_a p$, suggested in Pörn (1977):

$D'_a p$:   "p is dependent on a's action"
$C'_a p$:   "p is not independent of a's action".

Using this reading in (II.13) for $C'_a p$ yields the following: "if p is not independent of a's action then it is necessary for something a does that p is not independent of his action" (the consequent here could also be read: "... then p's being independent of a's action is incompatible with something a does").

In order to validate (II.13) in LC the following condition is added.

(Q.D+D′)   For all w, w_1, $w_2 \in W$, if $(w, w_1) \in R(D_a)$ and $(w, w_2) \in R(D'_a)$ then $(w_1, w_2) \in R(D'_a)$.

Thus, the addition of this condition, together with (Q.Trans) for $R(D_a)$, suffices to validate (II.9).

This discussion of (II.9) does not imply that (Q.Trans) should be adopted for $R(D'_a)$; there is good reason why this property should not be assigned to $R(D'_a)$, since it would validate (II.14) in LC:

(II.14) $D'_a p \rightarrow D'_a \sim D'_a p$;

(II.14) would seem to be unacceptable in the light of the proposed reading of the operator; furthermore, it can hardly be said that the intended interpretation of the relation $R(D'_a)$ carries a commitment to transitivity.

(I am inclined to think that the converse of (II.14) should be provable in LC — although little hinges on this as regards the purposes LC is intended to serve. Adoption of (Q.Euclid) for $R(D'_a)$ will enable this result to be secured.)

One further condition which connects $R(D_a)$ and $R(D'_a)$ will be adopted (*cf.* the condition (OM7.1) in Pörn, 1977, p. 6):

(Q.$R(D_a)$/$R(D'_a)$)) For all $w, w_1, w_2 \in W$, if $(w, w_1) \in R(D_a)$ and $(w_1, w_2) \in R(D'_a)$ then $(w, w_2) \in R(D'_a)$.

(II.15) will now be provable in LC:

(II.15) $D'_a p \rightarrow D_a D'_a p$

Since the converse of (II.15) also holds in LC, adoption of (Q.$R(D_a)$/$R(D'_a)$)) secures the result that p is dependent on a's action if and only if it is necessary for something a does that p is dependent on a's action. No further use will be made of this last condition; it is introduced merely to develop more fully the characterization of the components of the action logic.

The proposals here accepted for the logic of action may be summarized as follows: wffs of the form $E_a p$ are defined by (Df.E); C'_a is the dual of D'_a; for the logic of $D_a \in$ VM adopt (Q.M1), (Q.M2), (Q.Ref) and (Q.Trans); for the logic of $D'_a \in$ VM adopt (Q.M3), (Q.M4), (Q.Ser) and (Q.Euclid); relating the logics of the two component operators will be the two conditions (Q.D+D') and (Q.$R(D_a)$/$R(D'_a)$)).

Note that (R1) fails to hold for the logic of E_a, but that (R2) does hold:

(R2)   If $(p \leftrightarrow q)$ is a theorem of LC then $(E_a p \leftrightarrow E_a q)$ is a theorem of LC.

One feature of the logic of action which may seem *prima facie* puzzling is that (II.16) fails to be a theorem:

(II.16) $E_a(p \cdot q) \rightarrow (E_a p \cdot E_a q)$.

But note that the consequent of (II.16) implies that p is not independent of what a does *and* that q is not independent of what a does (in virtue of (Df.E)). However, application of (Df.E) to the antecedent of (II.16) yields $D_a(p \cdot q)$ and $C'_a(p \cdot q)$; according to the latter, the state of affairs described by p and q is not independent of a's action. But clearly this is compatible with the situation in which either p or q but not both *is* independent of a's action; q, perhaps, is true regardless of a's influence on the world. The truth of the antecedent of (II.16) requires merely that either $C'_a p$ or $C'_a q$ is true; thus, (II.17), but not (II.16), holds in LC:

(II.17) $E_a(p \cdot q) \rightarrow (E_a p \lor E_a q)$.

As regards the combination of the action modality with quantifiers, consider the following wffs of LC, $(F \in VP)$:

(II.18) $(x)E_a Fx \rightarrow E_a(x)Fx$
(II.19) $E_a(x)Fx \rightarrow (x)E_a Fx$
(II.20) $(\exists x)E_a Fx \rightarrow E_a(\exists x)Fx$
(II.21) $E_a(\exists x)Fx \rightarrow (\exists x)E_a Fx$.

It is well known that the way modalities mix with quantifiers within possible-world semantics is crucially dependent on assumptions about the transfer of individuals across accessible worlds. In LC, the only transfer assumption to be made is the following:

(Q.Q$^+$E)   for all $w, w_1 \in W$ and for any agent individual constant symbol b, if either $(w, w_1) \in R(D_b)$ or $(w, w_1) \in R(D'_b)$ then the individual denoted by b is a member of both $Q^+(w)$ and $Q^+(w_1)$.

This condition guarantees that an agent exists in the world in which he acts, and in all worlds praxiologically accessible to that world; (very little hinges on the adoption of this condition as regards the action logic's role in this essay).

(Q.Q$^+$E), in conjunction with the quantifier conditions and the conditions governing act descriptions, is insufficient to grant validity to *any* of (II.18)–(II.21), inclusive. (II.18), the action counterpart of the Barcan formula, would be valid if we made the following extra transfer assumption: for all $w, w_1 \in W$, if $(w, w_1) \in R(D_a)$ then $Q^+(w_1) \subseteq Q^+(w)$. For (II.19) to be valid it would be required that $Q^+(w) \subseteq Q^+(w_1)$, where $(w, w_1) \in R(D_a)$, but that would still not be sufficient to grant validity, because (II.22) is not (and clearly should not be) a theorem in LC:

(II.22) $C'_a(x)Fx \rightarrow (x)C'_aFx$

If the fact that everything has property F is not independent of a's action it does not follow from that that, for each individual, its having property F is not independent of a's action.

The D_a counterpart of (II.20) *is* a theorem in LC. (II.20) itself fails because (II.23) is not a theorem in LC:

(II.23) $(\exists x)C'_aFx \rightarrow C'_a(\exists x)Fx$

Suppose that a builds a car: then there is something such that its being a car is not independent of a's action. But it does not follow that *that* there exists something which is a car is not independent of a's action.

Finally, concerning the failure of (II.21), suppose it is true that a writes a message on a wall; it is by no means clear that it should follow from that that there is something such that a brings it about that *it* is a message written on a wall.

II.3 NORMATIVE MODALITIES

One aim of the present essay is to clarify the role of intention in the analysis of meaning and communication. Some means must be provided, therefore, whereby agents' intentions can be represented formally in LC. To this end, the modality Shall will be employed, as introduced in Pörn (1977); this modality will also figure in the account of non-declarative communication, since it seems clear that a prime function of such communication is that of setting tasks which shall be performed by those agents to whom such communications are addressed.

Detailed discussion of the use of this modality will be reserved until later; for the present, its definition can be stated as follows: Shall will not be understood as a relativized modality; wffs of the form Shall p and $\sim$Shall $\sim p$ will be evaluated by means of (Q.M1) and (Q.M2), respectively, with O_a in these conditions replaced throughout by Shall, and with the further proviso that the clause "and a denotes any agent individual in $Q^+(w)$" is to be eliminated from both (QM1) and (QM2). Wffs of the form Shall$p$ will be read: "it shall be the case that p". Wffs of the form $\sim$Shall $\sim p$ can be rewritten as May p and read: "it may be the case that p".

If $(w, w_1) \in$ R(Shall) then w_1 will be said to be normatively ideal relative to w and, by (QM1), it then follows that whatever *shall* be the case in w *is* the case in w_1. Similarly, given the equivalence of May p and $\sim$Shall $\sim p$, if May p obtains at w then, by (QM2), there is some normatively ideal version of w in which p itself obtains.

A measure of normative consistency may be imposed by adopting a condition of type (Q.Ser) for the relation R(Shall), in which case (II.24) will be valid in LC:

(II.24)   Shall $p \to$ May p.

It can readily be shown that both (R1) and (R2) hold in their Shall versions. That (R1) holds is less alarming than might at first be thought, given the intended role of the modality E_a within the scope of the Shall operator. In general, what is held to be normatively ideal is that such-and-such an act is performed − or at least that is how the modality Shall will be employed here. It has already been noted that (R1) fails to hold for E_a. (For further discussion of these issues see Pörn, 1977, Section 14, Pörn, 1974, Section 8, and the account of imperative inference, including treatment of Ross's paradox, in Section IV.3, below.)

II.4. THE BELIEF MODALITY

Let B_a designate the belief operator Hintikka used in his 1962 work on the logics of knowledge and belief. Adopting (Q.M1), (Q.M2), (Q.Ser), and (Q.Trans), replacing in them each occurrence of O_a by one of B_a, yields (quantification being ignored for the time being) semantics for Hintikka's original logic.

In this logic it is provably the case that all agents believe all logical truths and that they believe the logical consequences of that which they believe. Here, then, there is a problem comparable to that present in Pörn's original action logic; comparable, but not the same: for whereas it makes no sense to suppose that an agent brings about a logical truth, there is nothing wrong at all in supposing that an agent believes a logical truth; what is odd, of course, is that he provably believes all of them.

Hintikka (1962) contains discussion of this problem; two lines of solution are proposed, the second of which he adopts: (i) any wff of the form $B_a p$

should be read as: "it follows from what *a* believes that *p*" rather than as "*a* believes that *p*". Or, (ii) keep the reading of the operator as it is but drop the standard notion of consistency in favour of defensibility, so that instead of saying that a wff is valid, we say that its denial is indefensible; e.g., *a* would be in an indefensible position if he denied believing that *q*, given that he believed *p* and given that *q* is a logical consequence of *p*. However, dropping the standard metalogical notions would seem to be a high price to have to pay, and option (i), on the other hand, is disappointing, since what was wanted was a logic of belief, not of the consequences of beliefs.

Hintikka has given the name "the problem of logical omniscience" to that feature of his possible-world analysis of knowledge according to which it is provably the case that everyone always knows the logical consequences of what he knows. In more recent papers (e.g., Hintikka, 1979) he has described a new line of solution to the problem, employing a semantical framework derived from the theory of urn models. I choose here, however, not to adopt that line of approach to the belief counterpart of the problem of logical omniscience. Instead, I shall incorporate in LC the proposals made in Pörn, 1977, Section 11; they provide a viable solution to the above-mentioned difficulties by showing how to articulate what is involved in "... the sort of selective attention that is an obvious feature of belief" (*op. cit.*, p. 18).

The semantical conditions which will shortly be formulated are perhaps best understood in the light of the following remarks about (Q F) and (Q~) (p. 42): the latter require that, at each world *w*, any wff *p* is either assigned the value T or else assigned the value F; that is, the possibility is excluded that there is any world *w* such that *p* is not true at *w* and ~*p* is not true at *w*. The rule (Q~) requires that if *p* is not true then ~*p* is true, and it requires that if ~*p* is not true then *p* is true. Since, by (Q F), the truth of ~*p* at *w* means that *p* is false at *w*, the effect of (Q~) may be summed up by saying that it *forces* the truth or falsity of *p*, where *p* is any wff, in every world; in other words, the rule does not permit any truth-value "gap" of the type which would be allowed if it could consistently be said, of some world *w*, that, for some *p*, neither *p* nor its negation was true at *w*.

It will be by allowing truth-value gaps that provision will be made for the "selective attention" characteristic of belief. The structure of LC will be changed to that of the triple (V, Q, U), where U is a function whose properties will differ from those of Q precisely in regard to the question of truth-value gaps.

Let the function U^+ assign to each $w \in W$ a set of individuals: the individuals which are believed to be referents at w. $U^+(w)$ need not be identical with $Q^+(w)$, where w is any member of W, because it is possible that existing individuals are not believed to be referents, and it is possible to believe of some individual which does not exist that it is a referent. It is assumed, further, that with each member of $U^+(w)$ there is associated an individual constant symbol of which that member is believed to be the referent.

Let U^- be a function which assigns extensions to members of VP. Unlike Q^-, U^- need not be assumed to assign an extension to every member of VP at every member of W; but, if $N \in$ VP is a k-place predicate such that U^- assigns an extension to N at w, then $U^-(N, w) \subseteq (U^+(w))^k$, where $(U^+(w))^k$ is the set of all ordered k-tuples of individuals believed to be referents in w.

Condition (U N) can now be formulated thus:

(U N)   Where $(a_1, a_2, \ldots, a_k)$ is any sequence of k individual constant symbols, $U(N(a_1, a_2, \ldots, a_k), w) = T$ iff $U^-(N, w)$ contains the sequence of individuals believed to be designated by $(a_1, a_2, \ldots, a_k)$.

Where p is any *atomic* wff of LC, conditions (U$\sim$) and (U F) may be formulated as follows:

(U$\sim$)   If $U(\sim p, w) = T$ then $U(p, w) \neq T$.
(U F) $U(p, w) = F$ iff $U(\sim p, w) = T$.

For both the function Q and the function U the negation of an atomic wff is true if and only if the wff is itself false; and if an atomic wff is false then it is not true, and if it is true then it is not false; however, for the function U (unlike the function Q), if an atomic wff is not true it does not follow that it is false, and if an atomic wff is not false it does not follow that it is true. Thus, where p is any atomic wff and w is any world, the function U leaves open three possibilities: $U(p, w) = T$, or $U(\sim p, w) = T$, or both $U(p, w) \neq T$ and $U(\sim p, w) \neq T$. Of each of the first two possibilities it will be said that the atomic wff p *has a truth value* at w, and for the third possibility it will be said that p *lacks a truth value* at w.

The specification of the rules associated with the function U continues with the following conditions, which govern molecular or compound wffs (*cf.* Pörn, 1970, p. 20):

(Comp. 1)   A compound wff has a truth value at $w \in W$ iff all of its component wffs have a truth value at w.

(Comp. 2) If a compound wff has a truth value at $w \in W$, then the role of the truth-functional connectives in determining that truth value will be governed by the following conditions, where p, q are any wffs:

(U~~)   If $U(\sim\sim p, w) = T$ then $U(p, w) = T$

(U $\vee$)   If $U((p \vee q), w) = T$ then either
$U(p, w) = T$ or $U(q, w) = T$

(U $\cdot$)   If $U((p \cdot q), w) = T$ then $U(p, w) = T$ and
$U(q, w) = T$

(U~$\vee$)   If $U(\sim(p \vee q), w) = T$ then $U((\sim p \cdot \sim q), w) = T$

(U~ $\cdot$)   If $U(\sim(p \cdot q), w) = T$ then $U((\sim p \vee \sim q), w) = T$

(U $\rightarrow$)   If $U((p \rightarrow q), w) = T$ then $U((\sim p \vee q), w) = T$

(U~$\rightarrow$)   If $U(\sim(p \rightarrow q), w) = T$ then $U((p \cdot \sim q), w) = T$

(U $\leftrightarrow$)   If $U((p \leftrightarrow q), w) = T$ then either
$U((p \cdot q), w) = T$ or $U((\sim p \cdot \sim q), w) = T$

(U~$\leftrightarrow$)   If $U(\sim(p \leftrightarrow q), w) = T$ then either
$U((p \cdot \sim q), w) = T$ or $U((\sim p \cdot q), w) = T$

For quantified wffs the following rules are introduced:

(Comp. 3) A wff of the form $(x)p$ has a truth value at $w \in W$ iff $p(a/x)$ has a truth value at w for each individual constant symbol a of which some member of $U^+(w)$ is believed to be the referent. (Note that is has already been required that each member of $U^+(w)$ is associated with an individual constant symbol of which that member is believed to be the referent — see above, p. 54.)

(Comp. 4) A wff of the form $(\exists x)p$ has a truth value at $w \in W$ iff either $(x)p$ has a truth value at w or $U(p(a/x), w) = T$ for some individual constant symbol a of which some member of $U^+(w)$ is believed to be the referent.

(U U)   If $U((x)p, w) = T$ then $U(p(a/x), w) = T$ for every individual constant symbol a of which some member of $U^+(w)$ is believed to be the referent.

(U~U)   If $U(\sim(x)p, w) = T$ then $U((\exists x)\sim p, w) = T$.

(U$\exists$)   If $U((\exists x)p, w) = T$ then $U(p(a/x), w) = T$ for at least one individual constant symbol a of which some member of $U^+(w)$ is believed to be the referent.

(U~$\exists$)   If $U(\sim(\exists x)p, w) = T$ then $U((x)\sim p, w) = T$.

Modalized wffs are governed by (Comp. 5):

(Comp. 5)   A wff of the form $O_a p$ has a truth value at $w \in W$ iff p has a
truth value in all those worlds w_1 such that $(w, w_1) \in R(O_a)$,
where a denotes any agent individual in $U^+(w)$.

By way of illustration of the U conditions applicable to those modalized
wffs which do have truth values, consider (UM1) and (U~M1), which are the
U counterparts of (QM1):

(UM1)   If $U(O_a p, w) = T$ then $U(p, w_1) = T$ for all $w_1 \in W$ such that
$(w, w_1) \in R(O_a)$, where a denotes any agent individual in
$U^+(w)$.

(U~M1)   If $U(\sim O_a p, w) = T$ then $U(\sim p, w_1) = T$ for at least one
$w_1 \in W$ such that $(w, w_1) \in R(O_a)$, where a denotes any
agent individual in $U^+(w)$.

Now that the form of the conditions governing the U function has been
specified, LC's truth conditions for wffs of the form $B_a p$ may be formulated:

(QB) $Q(B_a p, w) = T$ iff $U(p, w_1) = T$ for all $w_1 \in W$ such that
$(w, w_1) \in R(B_a)$, where a denotes any agent individual in
$Q^+(w)$.

Note that this condition immediately yields the following for negated belief
formulae:

(Q~B) $Q(\sim B_a p, w) = T$ iff $U(p, w_1) \neq T$ for at least one $w_1 \in W$ such
that $(w, w_1) \in R(B_a)$, where a denotes any agent individual in
$Q^+(w)$.

Where $(w, w_1) \in R(B_a)$, w_1 may be understood intuitively as a kind of
idealization of w; it is an "ideal version" of w with respect to a's beliefs,
since what a believes to be the case in w is the case in w_1. Since belief does
not entail truth, it is obvious that the relation $R(B_a)$ is not reflexive. However,
(Q.Ser) is adopted for $R(B_a)$, with the consequence that what a believes in
w is true in at least one ideal version of w, and hence with the further consequence that (II.25) is a theorem of LC:

(II.25) $B_a p \rightarrow \sim B_a \sim p$.

The way in which this logic of belief copes with the kinds of difficulties which were described earlier in this section may be brought out by considering the abortive attempt to construct a proof of (II.26):

(II.26) $B_a p \rightarrow B_a(p \vee q)$.

(Hintikka's original belief logic of course validated (II.26), since $(p \vee q)$ is a logical consequence of p.) Suppose that there is some $w \in W$ such that:

1. $Q(\sim(B_a p \rightarrow B_a(p \vee q)), w) = T$

then, $\begin{cases} 2.\ Q(B_a p, w) = T \\ \text{from } 1 \ | \ 3.\ Q(\sim B_a(p \vee q), w) = T \end{cases}$ $\begin{array}{l} \text{by } (Q\sim) \text{ and } (Q\sim\sim) \text{ and} \\ (Q\rightarrow) \end{array}$

from 3, 4. $U((p \vee q), w_1) \neq T$ for some $w_1 \in W$ such that

$(w, w_1) \in R(B_a)$; by $(Q\sim B)$.

from 2, 5. $U(p, w_1) = T$, by (QB), since $(w, w_1) \in R(B_a)$.

The next step is to consider whether the wff $(p \vee q)$ has a truth value at w_1; all that is known so far is that it is not true. The condition (Comp. 1) says that it has a truth value at w_1 provided that each of its component wffs has a truth value at w_1. Line 5 of the proof shows that p has a truth value at that world, but it is clear that there are no grounds for concluding that q also has a truth value there. So the proof can proceed no further; the denial of (II.26) has not be shown to be a contradiction, and therefore (II.26) has not been shown to be a theorem.

Note that were it the case, at w, either that a believes that q or that a believes that $\sim q$, then q would have a truth value at w_1 (for either q or its negation would then be true at w_1, by (QB)); but in fact nothing is known about whether a has any beliefs about q — so q lacks a truth value at w_1. Again it can be seen here how the logic captures the notion of "selective attention" which is characteristic of belief.

It is clear from the above that $B_a p$ does entail $B_a(p \vee q)$ if either $B_a q$ or $B_a \sim q$; furthermore, it is easy to see how it can be shown that $B_a p$ entails $B_a(p \vee \sim p)$. These observations point to the following generalization: that whether a wff $B_a q$ is a logical consequence of some set of beliefs $\{B_a p, B_a p_1, \ldots, B_a p_n\}$ is going to depend on whether the scope of that set of a's beliefs "covers" q; for a precise statement of that generalization, including a definition of the idea that one set of wffs "covers" another, the reader is referred to Pörn, 1977, p. 21.

Note, also, that there will be no theorems of the form $B_a p$, where p is any wff; thus it will not be *provably* the case, of any agent, that he believes any logical truths. For example, the attempt to show that the denial of

$B_a(p \lor \sim p)$ is contradictory, at some $w \in W$, is soon seen to be abortive: given that $Q(\sim B_a(p \lor \sim p), w) = T$, it follows by $(Q \sim B)$ that $U((p \lor \sim p), w_1) \neq T$ for some $w_1 \in W$ such that $(w, w_1) \in R(B_a)$. But there the proof can proceed no further, except on the assumption that p does have a truth value at w_1.

Among the features which the present logic *shares* with Hintikka's original logic of belief, are those represented by (II.27) and (II.28), below, both of which are theorems:

(II.27) $(B_a p \cdot B_a(p \to q)) \to B_a q$
(II.28) $(B_a p \cdot B_a q) \to B_a(p \cdot q)$.

The basic properties of the quantified belief logic are revealed by the fact that, of (II.29)–(II.32) below, only (II.31) is valid in LC; $(F \in VP)$:

(II.29) $(x)B_a Fx \to B_a(x)Fx$
(II.30) $B_a(x)Fx \to (x)B_a Fx$
(II.31) $(\exists x)B_a Fx \to B_a(\exists x)Fx$
(II.32) $B_a(\exists x)Fx \to (\exists x)B_a Fx$.

Some comments are in order concerning (II.30) and (II.31). Application of the *reductio* proof strategy already outlined to the case of (II.30) yields, in a few steps, that $Q(B_a(x)Fx, w) = T$ and $Q(\sim B_a Fb, w) = T$, where b is an individual constant symbol. Hence $U(Fb, w_1) \neq T$ and $U((x)Fx, w_1) = T$ for some $w_1 \in W$ such that $(w, w_1) \in R(B_a)$; but the proof proceeds no further: in particular, note that the move cannot be made from $U((x)Fx, w_1) = T$ to $U(Fb, w_1) = T$ given that no assumption has been made to the effect that, where $(w, w_1) \in R(B_a)$, $Q^+(w) \subseteq U^+(w_1)$; and it is clear that an assumption of this sort should not be made, because the fact that an individual exists at w does not entail that it is taken to exist in each doxastically ideal version of w. As regards (II.31), the *reductio* strategy yields $Q(\sim B_a(\exists x)Fx, w) = T$ and $Q(B_a Fb, w) = T$, where b is an individual constant symbol. Then $U((\exists x)Fx, w_1) \neq T$ and $U(Fb, w_1) = T$ for some w_1 such that $(w, w_1) \in R(B_a)$. By (Comp. 4) it now follows that $(\exists x)Fx$ has a truth value at w_1, because U assigns the value T to Fb at w_1. It is now obvious that a contradiction arises whichever of the two truth values $(\exists x)Fx$ takes at w_1.

Finally, one further comparison with Hintikka's (1962) logic of belief, in which either the relation of doxastic alternativeness was required to be transitive or else it was stipulated that an agent believes at least as much in the doxastic alternatives to a world w as he does in w itself. The fact that

Hintikka adopted one of these two conditions meant that (II.33) was provable in his system:

(II.33) $B_a p \rightarrow B_a B_a p$.

I am not convinced by Hintikka's arguments in defence of (II.33); it seems to me that the most useful role played in his logic by the requirement of transitivity of the relation (or the "equivalent" condition) is that it provides the key move in the proof of the indefensibility of wffs of the form $B_a(p \cdot \sim B_a p)$ — and this, in turn, is the crux of Hintikka's treatment of Moore's paradox of saying and disbelieving. I later provide a different diagnosis of that paradox, and show how the puzzle can be explained without recourse to semantical conditions of the type which generate (II.33) in the class of valid wffs; (see below, Section III.2). However, it will also be suggested later that perhaps both (II.33) and its converse should be considered to be true in all those situations which, relative to a given situation, are deontically ideal in a certain sense. It will be the aim of Section II.7 to specify which particular notion of deontic ideality that is.

II.5. MUTUAL BELIEF

In Chapter I it was maintained that the analysis of interpersonal communication requires reference to beliefs mutually held by communicator and audience; the present section provides a means of characterizing mutual belief: let it first be stated explicitly, then, that the syntax of LC will be extended so that, where p is any wff of LC and a and b are agent individual variable or constant symbols of LC, then $B_{ab}^* p$ is a wff of LC, to be read "a and b mutually believe that p".

If a and b mutually believe that p then a believes that b believes that p, b believes that a believes that p, a believes that b believes that a believes that p ... and so on. It is by no means inconceivable that a and b mutually believe that p without it being the case either that a believes that p or that b believes that p. But having admitted that, I want to add that the cases in which a and b mutually believe that p without (either of them) actually believing that p individually will prove to be of no interest in the description of those aspects of communication with which the present work is concerned. I therefore choose to exclude such cases at the outset; if a and b mutually believe that p it will follow, according to the definition here to be offered, that each individually believes that p.

Truth conditions for wffs of the type $B_{ab}^* p$ are given by condition (Q.B*):

(Q.B*)   Where w is any member of W and a and b denote any agent individuals in w, then $Q(B^*_{ab}p, w) = T$ iff Q assigns the value T at w to each wff in the set of wffs $\{B^*_{ab}\}$. The set $\{B^*_{ab}\}$ is defined as follows:

(i) $B_a p$ is a member of $\{B^*_{ab}\}$;

(ii) $B_b p$ is a member of $\{B^*_{ab}\}$;

(iii)   if q is any member of $\{B^*_{ab}\}$ whose left-most belief operator has subscript a, then $B_b q$ is a member of $\{B^*_{ab}\}$;

(iv)   if q is any member of $\{B^*_{ab}\}$ whose left-most belief operator has subscript b, then $B_a q$ is a member of $\{B^*_{ab}\}$;

(v)   no wff is a member of $\{B^*_{ab}\}$ unless its being so is guaranteed by the conditions (i), (ii), (iii), (iv).

Some might wish to maintain that if a wff contains more than m iterations of belief operators it is unintelligible; in which case let them decide upon a value for m and build that into the definition of $B^*_{ab}p$.

The specification of appropriate U conditions for wffs expressing mutual beliefs should now be a routine matter; I omit the formal details here, since I shall not in fact be concerned with examples (for present purposes) in which reference is made to the beliefs some agent c may be supposed to have about the mutual beliefs held by a and b.

II.6. THE MODALITY V_a

V_a is a member of VM, and wffs of the form $V_a p$ are read "according to the information available to a, p is true". This reading is somewhat cumbersome, and it lacks precision. It is the task of this section (and the next) to try to specify the intended interpretation of the operator as clearly as possible.

Truth conditions for wffs of the type $V_a p$ take the same form as those used for the belief modality:

(QV) $Q(V_a p, w) = T$ iff $U(p, w_1) = T$ for all $w_1 \in W$ such that $(w, w_1) \in R(V_a)$, where a denotes any agent individual in $Q^+(w)$.

This condition entails condition (Q~V), which is formulated by replacing every occurrence of B_a in (Q~B) by one of V_a. The function U evaluates wffs of the forms $V_a p$ and $\sim V_a p$ in accordance with the rules (UM1) and (U~M1) — see above, p. 56 — there replacing each occurrence of O_a by one of V_a.

Resort to the use of the function U in specifying truth conditions for wffs exhibiting this operator is justified by appeal to the fact that the "selective attention" of an agent plays a role in determining what, *according to the information available to him*, is true — just as it also plays a role in determining what he believes; that this is so should become clearer from the discussion which follows.

What is to be meant by the claim that a pair of worlds, (w, w_1), is a member of $R(V_a)$? How is that relation to be understood? Imagine individual a at w: it may be supposed that a has available to him, at w, a body of information in the light of which he might be able to try, if he so wishes, to make an assessment of whether or not the state of affairs described by p obtains at w. The use a makes of the available information will be selective; some bits of information might be ignored by him completely; there may be some bits of information which he considers only if he also considers certain other bits: it is obvious that there are likely to be *various* kinds of factors at work in determining which patterns of selection of the available information are adopted. And it is also obvious that the content of the body of information said to be "available" to a will be delimited by what a — viewed as an information receiver — is able to register.

But just suppose that a does consider whether, on the basis of the information available to him, p is true; how is that situation to be characterized? The intuition behind the use here made of the relation $R(V_a)$ is that a's considering whether p is true may itself be seen as an activity of a in which he selects and processes extracts, or samples, of the information which is available to him. Thus, where $(w, w_1) \in R(V_a)$, the world w_1 is the world described by a processed sample of the information available to a at w — it being understood that it is a who has done the sampling and the processing. Consequently, the import of the condition (QV) is essentially this: if p is true according to *each one* of the processed samples a produces from the body of information available to him at w, then (at w) p will be true according to the information available to a.

It is important to stress that the truth of $V_a p$ at w is *not* here taken to entail that p is required to be true *no matter how* the information available to a at w is sampled and processed; the possibility is left entirely open that a has adopted one out of several conceivable strategies or procedures for sampling, and that had he adopted a different sampling procedure $V_a p$ (at w) would have turned out to be false. The way in which a samples the body of information available to him is one aspect of the *enquiring system* he implements; the way in which he *processes* the samples is another aspect of that enquiring system: thus, whether or not a particular sample of information "requires" the truth of p will depend upon the way in which the information is processed, i.e., on the canons of evidence and the rules of inference which are employed.

No assumption is here made to the effect that an agent must be fully aware of the nature of the sampling and processing procedures he employs; and no assumption is made to the effect that a samples and processes in accordance with some independently specified norms for correctness, reliability or accuracy.

One consequence of this last point is that b's believing that $V_a p$ provides b with good grounds for believing that p only if b can be sure *both* that a has access to the relevant information *and* that a adopts reliable procedures for sampling and processing that information. This, of course, corresponds to the situation in real life: whether or not an agent $-$ *qua* source of information $-$ can be relied upon depends, in part, on the nature of the enquiring system he employs. That factors of this sort are implicit in the account of the operator V_a is relevant to the characterization of audience trust given in Section III.1.

In order to make factors of this kind *explicit* in the formal model, some means would have to be found of characterizing agents in terms of the enquiring systems they implement; some additional formal tools from cybernetic theory $-$ to mention one source $-$ would be called for. (This task is beyond the scope of the present essay, but would appear to represent an interesting line of further development. It might constitute a possible means of linking the description of communication with the description of personality $-$ *if* it is reasonable to make the assumption that the kind of person an agent is might be given a partial characterization by reference to the kinds of enquiring systems he implements.)

The above account of the relation $R(V_a)$ indicates that it is not to be assigned the property of reflexivity; it is appropriate, however, that it be made a serial relation: in the light of the intuitive understanding of the relation, the adoption of (Q.Ser) amounts to the assumption that no matter which situation an agent is in he is always engaged to some degree in the task of sampling and processing the information available to him. (II.34) now joins the class of theorems of LC:

(II.34) $V_a p \rightarrow \sim V_a \sim p$.

The validity of (II.34) should not be thought to prevent the logic from expressing the idea that inconsistencies may arise within what, according to the information available to a, is true. For the logic allows that the conjunction of $V_a p$ and $V_a q$ may be true even when $\sim p$ is a logical consequence of q (*cf.* Pörn, 1977, pp. 20–21, on the analogous point in the logic of belief).

The following wffs, *none* of which is provable in LC, express links between the modalities V_a and B_a:

(II.35) $V_a p \to B_a p$

(II.36) $V_a p \to \sim B_a \sim p$

(II.37) $B_a p \to V_a p$.

The absence of (II.35) from the class of theorems of LC means that, although p may be true according to the information available to a, a might still not accept that p is true: a might not be convinced that the evidence available to him is adequate to justify his believing that p. Furthermore, since (II.37) is not provable, it follows that a may believe that p without its being the case that p is true according to the information available to him. It happens, as a plain matter of fact, that some agents hold beliefs for which their own enquiring systems fail to provide them with evidence, and that they may even hold beliefs which fly in the face of the information available to them (as is reflected by the failure of (II.36) to be a theorem).

It may be suggested, however, that in "ideal circumstances" each of the above wffs should hold; the next section contains a characterization of a concept of ideality in terms of which some optimal relationships between believing and having evidence may be specified. These relationships will be optimal relative to a particular interest agents have — namely, their interest in being informed.

II.7. DEONTIC MODALITIES

For a given agent a, at w, it may be that certain states of affairs are optimal or ideal — that is, it may be that some particular states of affairs best meet his interests.

Thus, relative to agent a, there may be ideal versions of w in which everything which is optimal for him in w, or everything which best meets his interests in w, in fact obtains. Where w_1 is such a world, (w, w_1) will be a member of $R(O_a)$, and wffs of the types $O_a p$ and $\sim O_a \sim p$ will be given truth conditions in the form of (Q.M1) and (Q.M2), respectively, replacing each occurrence of O_a in (Q.M1) and (Q.M2) by one of O_a. Since what best meets a's interests at w might not in fact obtain at w, the relation $R(O_a)$ will not be assigned the property of reflexivity. Any world might fail to be an ideal version of itself relative to a. However, it will be assumed that for every world w there is an ideal version of it: that is, (Q.Ser) will be adopted for R(O_a), thereby guaranteeing that (II.38) is a theorem of LC:

(II.38) $O_a p \to \sim O_a \sim p$.

In some respects the semantical conditions governing the modalities O_a and Shall are alike; and for both of the relations R(O_a) and R(Shall) the second terms of those ordered pairs which are members of these relations may be described as ideal versions of the first terms; but they are ideal versions of distinct types and it is vitally important that the distinction be kept clear. That only one of the two modalities is relativized is but a minor difference; the important differences may be brought out in this way: following Pörn (1977) (see especially Section 13), one particular use to which the Shall modality will be put is exhibited in wffs (II.39) and (II.40):

(II.39) $B_a(p \to$ Shall $E_a q)$
(II.40) $B_b(p \to$ Shall $E_a q)$;

(II.39) is read: "a intends to bring it about that q if p" and (II.40) is read: "b expects a to bring it about that q if p". (The kind of expectation b has of a according to (II.40) is compatible with b's believing that a will not *in fact* do q if p obtains. Lord Nelson might have expected every man to do his duty without also believing that any of them would.) Compare (II.39) with (II.41) and (II.40) with (II.42):

(II.41) $B_a(p \to O_a E_a q)$
(II.42) $B_b(p \to O_a E_a q)$;

(II.39) and (II.41) are logically independent; a might believe that if p, then it best meets his interests that he does q, without intending to do q if p. And he may intend to do q if p without believing that, if p, then it best meets his interests that he does q. Furthermore, (II.40) and (II.42) are logically independent; b might expect of a that he does q if p obtains without also believing that, if p, it best meets a's interests that a does q. And b might believe that, if p, then it best meets a's interests that a does q without expecting of a that a does q if p obtains.

Some further discussion of the distinction between these two modalities is contained in Pörn, 1977, Section 18, where he points out, following Kanger (1972), that the only logical connection which seems to be required between them is that the relation R(O_a) be a subset of the relative product

$R(O_a)/R(\text{Shall})$. Accepting this point, and adopting this condition, LC now validates wffs of the following type:

(II.43) $O_a \text{Shall} E_a p \rightarrow O_a E_a p$.

Given the role assigned to the modality Shall in the analysis of intention, it is clear that the distinction between the normative and deontic modalities is of relevance to the characterization of rules of information and to the criticism of Grice and Lewis. To that issue I return in Chapter V.

The properties discussed so far in this section hold for wffs of the type $O_a p$ regardless of which specific type of interest of a one has in mind when reading them as "it best meets a's interests that p". However, the intended interpretation of wffs of this sort in LC will pertain to a specific type of interest of a — namely, his interest in being *informed*. In order to reflect this intended interpretation through the semantical conditions governing LC, certain links will be specified between the modality O_a and the modalities B_a and V_a; it would not be appropriate to adopt the extra semantical conditions which now follow unless it was intended that the interest of a with which we are here concerned is his interest in being informed.

The earlier discussion of the logic of V_a explains why the truth of p is not entailed by the truth of $V_a p$; however, it will be made a characteristic feature of those circumstances which are ideal or optimal relative to a's interest in being informed that, in such circumstances, the truth of p is guaranteed if p is true according to the information available to a. Hence (II.44) will be a theorem of LC, and this result will be secured by adopting the condition $(QO_a V_a 1)$:

(II.44) $O_a(V_a p \rightarrow p)$;
$(QO_a V_a 1)$ For all $w, w_1 \in W$, if $(w, w_1) \in R(O_a)$ then $(w_1, w_1) \in R(V_a)$.

In virtue of the logic of O_a, (II.45) is derivable from (II.44):

(II.45) $O_a V_a p \rightarrow O_a p$.

The relationship between the modalities O_a and V_a will be strengthened yet further by requiring the provability of (II.46):

(II.46) $O_a V_a p \rightarrow p$.

(II.46) will be provable when $(QO_a V_a 2)$ is added to the set of semantical conditions:

(QO_aV_a2) For all $w \in W$ there is some $w_1 \in W$ such that (w, w_1)
$\in R(O_a)$ and $(w_1, w) \in R(V_a)$.

In the light of the earlier discussion of the way in which the modality V_a
(and its associated accessibility relation) are to be understood, theorems
(II.44)–(II.46) may be seen as specifying conditions under which it would
be true to say that a is operating an enquiring system which, relative to his
interest in being informed, is functioning optimally.

It was hinted at the end of Section II.6 that the characterization of the
modality O_a would include the specification of a relationship between
believing and having evidence. In fact the requirement which will now be
imposed is that wffs of the forms B_ap and V_ap will be provably equivalent
in all those situations which, relative to some situation w, are ideal relative to
a's interest in being informed. Thus, in such situations, a believes that p only
if p is true according to the information available to him, and he believes that
p if p is true according to the information available to him. The provability
of (II.47) and (II.48) is secured by means of the addition of $(QO_aV_aB_a)$
to the set of semantical conditions:

(II.47) $O_a(V_ap \to B_ap)$
(II.48) $O_a(B_ap \to V_ap)$
$(QO_aV_aB_a)$ For all w, w_1, $w_2 \in W$, if $(w, w_1) \in R(O_a)$ then $(w_1,$
$w_2) \in R(V_a)$ if and only if $(w_1, w_2) \in R(B_a)$.

It should be emphasized that the point behind the adoption of the last
three semantical conditions is to develop the explicit statement of the intended interpretation of the deontic operator by indicating its place within a
small network of operators, thereby removing, to some degree, the vagueness
inherent in the reading given to the operator in English; alternatively, it may
be said that the conditions serve the purpose of stating more precisely just
what it is for a situation to be "ideal relative to an agent's interest in being
informed".

It is obvious that (II.49), (II.50), and (II.51) will be further consequences
of the new conditions:

(II.49) $O_a(V_ap \to \sim B_a \sim p)$
(II.50) $O_a(B_ap \to p)$
(II.51) $O_a B_ap \to p.$

As an instance of (II.50) it is clear that (II.52) — and its counterpart for the
modality V_a — will be provable:

(II.52) $O_a(B_aB_ap \rightarrow B_ap)$.

(II.52) prompts consideration of the further question as to whether the semantical distinction between wffs of the form B_ap and B_aB_ap should disappear in all those worlds which, relative to a's interest in being informed, are ideal versions of a given world; (and likewise for wffs of the forms V_ap and V_aV_ap). My inclination is to answer the question in the affirmative, and thus to require that what was perhaps the most striking characteristic of Hintikka's logic of belief — that a's believing that p entails that a believes that he believes that p — should hold in all those situations which are optimal relative to a's interest in being informed. Hence, (II.53) will be provable:

(II.53) $O_a(B_ap \rightarrow B_aB_ap)$.

Accordingly, the property of transitivity is assigned to the appropriate subset of the set of ordered pairs which comprise $R(B_a)$; this new condition must, however, be carefully restricted lest — in combination with the others — it validates (II.54)–(II.57), none of which are acceptable as theorems of LC:

(II.54) $O_aB_ap \rightarrow B_ap$
(II.55) $O_aB_ap \rightarrow V_ap$
(II.56) $O_aV_ap \rightarrow V_ap$
(II.57) $O_aV_ap \rightarrow B_ap$.

The more general point to be made in connection with (II.54) and (II.56) is that there will be *no* instances of (II.58) among the class of theorems of LC:

(II.58) $O_ap \rightarrow p$;

that p is optimal — relative to a's interest in being informed — at some world does not entail that p is true at that world, no matter which state of affairs is described by p.

To see why the converse of (II.58) should fail to be provable, consider a case in which p takes the form E_bq, and suppose further that this act of b is a signalling act which a and b (mutually) believe means that r; any instance in which b brings it about that q even though, according to the information available to him, r is false, will be an instance in which O_aE_bq is false.

Finally, consider wffs (II.59) and (II.60):

(II.59) $O_a(p \rightarrow B_ap)$
(II.60) $p \rightarrow O_aB_ap$.

It might be said, concerning (II.59), that it should be in the class of theorems of LC: for, surely, it is optimal, relative to a's interest in being informed, that he believes that p if p is true. However, that interpretation of the notion of optimality carries the assumption that it is ideal that an agent's information is *complete* – in the sense that, under optimal conditions, he accepts as true every truth. But why make an assumption of that sort? Given that the human agent's information storage capacity is not unlimited, the assumption amounts to the adoption of an ideal which is in fact unreachable by the human; but even if one overlooks that point, there is still no good reason to insist that a's beliefs would meet optimal standards only if they were complete in this sense. The question of *how much* true information a must be required to accept as true (under circumstances which are optimal relative to his interest in being informed) is here left entirely open, the only exception being the case represented by (II.53), the validity of which requires completeness of a's beliefs *about what he believes* – surely desirable of human enquiring systems – in all such ideal circumstances.

That completes the acount of the deontic modality; in conclusion, it is worth emphasizing the point that, given the earlier intuitive characterization of the relation $R(V_a)$, the stipulated relationship between the relations $R(V_a)$ and $R(O_a)$ provides a partial specification of what it would be for a's enquiring system to be functioning optimally. Similarly, where p – in a wff of type $O_a p$ – takes the form $E_b q$, and the act concerned is of a type which figures in a signalling system (verbal or non-verbal) used by a and b, it may be said that $O_a E_b q$ will be true just of those situations in which a performance by b of the signalling act would count as optimal usage of the signalling system; a's enquiring system functions optimally if the information it supplies him is true; a signalling system used by a and b functions optimally when it is used in such a way that, in giving a signal, b enables a to determine how things stand according to the information available to b. It is a central feature of LC that one and the same modality may be employed to characterize, at least partially, the optimal functioning of both enquiring systems and signalling systems.

II.8. KNOWLEDGE THAT p

The modalities O_a, V_a and B_a provide a possible basis for the definition of wffs of the form $K_a p$, where these are read: "a knows that p". The proposal here to be made is as follows:

(Df.K) $K_a p =_{df} (B_a p \cdot V_a p \cdot O_a V_a p)$.

According to (Df.K), a's knowing that p amounts to this: a accepts that p is true (he believes that p); p is true according to the information available to a; and it is optimal, relative to a's interest in being informed, that, according to the information available to him, p is true. In virtue of the validity of (II.46), (Df.K) guarantees that $K_a p$ entails that p.

As Pörn points out (1977, pp. 107–8), the claim that a deontic element of some sort figures in the analysis of sentences of the form "a knows that p" is by no means new; so (Df.K) represents one way in which a claim of that sort might be elaborated. Whether or not true opinion counts as knowledge "depends on the reliability of the enquiring system used to collect the evidence" (Pörn, *loc. cit.*). On my account, a's accepting p as true counts as knowledge that p given (i) that p is true according to the information available to him and (ii) that p's being true according to the information available to him is sufficient to guarantee the truth of p; (ii) holds provided that a implements an enquiring system which meets optimal standards — optimal in the sense described by the modality O_a — at least with respect to the task of determining the truth value of p.

II.9. ON THE ALLEGED CIRCULARITY OF POSSIBLE-WORLD SEMANTICS

The characterizations given to the modalities contained in LC do exhibit circularity. The truth of $B_a p$ at w requires the truth of p in all those worlds w_1 which are ideal versions of w relative to a's *beliefs*; the truth of $E_a p$ at w requires the truth of $C'_a p$ at w, which in turn requires the falsity of p in some situation in which a does not *do* all of the things which he *does* in w; the truth of Shall p at w requires the truth of p in all normatively ideal versions of w . . . and so on.

It is a mistake, however, to draw the conclusion that this form of circularity renders unacceptable this kind of approach to the logic of modalities. "The circle is not a vicious one . . . but is so large as to bring out a great deal of important structure of our modal concepts" (Hintikka, 1979, p. 367; and *cf.* Pörn, 1977, p. 13). The framework provided by possible-world semantics is rich enough and flexible enough to permit precise specification of some of the key principles involved in reasoning about belief, action and the other modalities in LC. From the outset, the task was to construct a logic — a means of examining systematically relations of entailment between sentences exhibiting modalities of these kinds; that task is in no way vitiated by the above-mentioned circularity. Had the task been to attempt to *reduce* these modal notions to some other notions then, of course, it would have been appropriate to describe the circle as vicious; but the aim was not to carry out reductions of this sort: indeed for some, at least, of the modalities in LC the philosophical literature provides ample grounds for doubting whether such reductions can be effected.

As regards the properties of the various accessibility relations, the procedure followed, in general, was to determine them in the light of considering which formulae were wanted in the class of theorems which express the basic characteristics of the modalities and their inter-relationships. Again, it would be a mistake to maintain that a procedure of this kind is vitiated by circularity; if, for example, one is convinced that there is no semantical distinction to be drawn between wffs of forms $E_a p$ and $E_a E_a p$ then one arranges the properties of the accessibility relations $R(D_a)$ and $R(D'_a)$ — including the relations between those relations — accordingly. Likewise, concerning the modality O_a, I fixed the relationship between $R(O_a)$ and $R(B_a)$ so that (II.50), for example, was provable just because that was a characteristic feature of the concept of ideality I was trying to articulate.

It is also worth repeating, in this connection, that an important aspect of the way the modalities are characterized is that they are set in relation to each other; each forms an element in a network of concepts.

My impression is that the charges of vicious circularity are rooted in presuppositions concerning the purpose which the possible-world analysis, *qua* philosophical analysis, ought to be serving; these presuppositions pertain to what is supposed to be acceptable as genuinely *philosophical* analysis. For example, it would seem to be taken for granted by a number of philosophers that the *central* concern of a truly *philosophical* analysis of belief would be an "in depth" examination of the concept, including investigation of the possibility of reducing that concept to some other(s). Formal techniques would then be properly employed as tools in the service of philosophical enquiry only to the extent that they helped reveal insights into these depths.

Perhaps the conclusion to be drawn is that the present essay in applied modal logic is not properly described as an essay in philosophical analysis. I would lose no sleep over that conclusion, even if it were true. It should, however, be pointed out that philosophers of language who have concerned themselves with the theory of speech acts have been essentially preoccupied with problems of describing aspects of social interaction — with problems of characterizing the types of beliefs and intentions agents have in virtue of which communication becomes possible; their task has been no different from the one taken up in this essay: but here techniques of modal logic have been employed in order to provide the means for *systematic* and *precise* description of the relevant beliefs and intentions, and in order to facilitate investigation of entailment relations between these descriptions.

It seems clear that the use here made of formal techniques is directly comparable to, for example, the use to which graph theory has been put in the description of the structure of human groups (see, e.g., Doreian, 1970). But who would accuse the social psychologist or sociologist of "circularity" in his use of graph-theoretical techniques, on the grounds that he deliberately builds into his formal model structures appropriate for portraying what he takes to be the salient features of the kinds of groups he is investigating? It would be preposterous to level an accusation of that kind, and it is just as silly to raise it against the present essay. It is apparent that a number of the issues taken up in the literature on the theory of speech acts are indistinguishable from topics in descriptive social psychology: and it should be equally apparent that there is a dire need for formal tools adequate for that descriptive task; modal logic can supply some of these.

What, then, are the criteria in terms of which the adequacy of LC is to be assessed? In addition to the obvious requirement of internal consistency, the language is to be evaluated in terms of its expressive capacity. Since LC is designed for the task of describing certain key aspects of situations in which agents communicate with one another, arguments which count against LC are arguments which show that there are important aspects of such interaction situations which fall beyond LC's descriptive capacity — that, for example, there are theoretically valuable distinctions which LC is unable to express. Furthermore, considerations of simplicity and economy are important: if it could be shown, for instance, that expressions having essentially the same role (in the theory) as my rules of information *could* have been formulated without the use of the modality O_a — perhaps with the use of Shall instead — then that would constitute a powerful argument against LC; and an argument of that sort, if it could be substantiated, would carry further consequences for the assessment of the Gricean type of approach (*cf.* below, Chapter V).

CHAPTER III

SOME FEATURES OF COMMUNICATION SITUATIONS

III.1. TRUTHFULNESS AND TRUST

Lewis is right, I believe, in assigning a key role to truthfulness and trust in the description of interpersonal communication. But some of the argument in Chapter I was designed to show that the role he chooses for these notions is the wrong one; an account was there proposed, both of meaning and of what it is for an act to be established in a population as a bearer of meaning, which left open the possibility that the members of a population are not regularly truthful and trusting in their use of language and signalling systems. That there is a need for such an alternative account to Lewis's stems from the fact that a great deal of communication goes on against a background of dishonesty and suspicion, and from what would seem to be the reasonable hypothesis that *one and the same* language or signalling system can be used in both an atmosphere of mutual trust and an atmosphere of mutual suspicion. Use of a language (or signalling system) involves the employment of a set of meaning-bearing devices; it is my contention that if truthfulness and trust are not made constitutive of language (or signalling system) use – if it is not *required* by the theory that the members of the language/signalling system-using population are regularly truthful and trusting – then a more flexible and realistic picture of what goes on in communication situations may be presented; and this picture may be more sensitive to the manifold ways in which meaning-bearing devices may be exploited.

This section now maps out with more formal detail, and exemplifies more fully, distinctions already mentioned in Chapter I.

Suppose that the mutual belief described by (III.1) is held by any two agents a and b: ((III.1) = (I.25))

$$\text{(III.1)} \quad B^*_{ab}((E_b p \cdot Z) \cdot O_a(E_b p \cdot Z)) \rightarrow V_b q);$$

then, as was argued in Chapter I, it follows that a believes that any non-deceiving performance (in circumstances Z) of the act described by $E_b p$ is a sign that, according to the information available to b, q is true. This, in turn, entails that a believes that b's doing p in circumstances Z means that q.

Suppose further that (III.2) is true:

(III.2) $B_a(E_b p \cdot Z)$;

so a believes that the performance, in Z, has occurred. a is said to take the performance as non-deceiving if not only (III.2) but also (III.3) is true:

(III.3) $B_a O_a(E_b p \cdot Z)$;

The joint truth of (III.2) and (III.3) characterizes one species of audience trust in the communicator's performance.

By the logic of belief (III.2) and (III.3) together entail (III.4), and by the logic of mutual belief (III.1) entails (III.5):

(III.4) $B_a((E_b p \cdot Z) \cdot O_a(E_b p \cdot Z))$
(III.5) $B_a(((E_b p \cdot Z) \cdot O_a(E_b p \cdot Z)) \rightarrow V_b q)$.

Furthermore, (III.6) is entailed by the conjunction of (III.4) and (III.5):

(III.6) $B_a V_b q$.

So, given (III.1), if a believes that a non-deceiving performance (in circumstances Z) of the act described by $E_b p$ has occurred then a believes that, according to the information available to b, q is true.

As was noted in passing in Chapter I, (III.6) does not entail that a believes that b believes that q. It is important to see that a's belief that b is insincere, in the sense shortly to be defined, does not necessarily provide a with good grounds for refusing to accept the performance as non-deceiving. For it is quite conceivable that a is correct in thinking that b is non-deceivingly reporting on how things stand *according to the information available to him* (b), even though he (a) might also be correct in supposing that b himself has not found that information adequate to justify his (b's) believing that it is true.

Just what the grounds are on which an audience *is* likely to judge whether or not a communicator's performance is non-deceiving is an issue to which I shall return in due course.

Cases in which the communicator's act is not of the non-deceiving type — and/or in which the audience does not believe it to be non-deceiving — are, of course, commonplace. But it is surely equally clear that such cases constitute violation of any supposed convention of truthfulness or convention of trust (or violation of both), and yet they clearly represent use of language (or signalling system); but the means are available here for describing what goes on in such situations.

There are uses of language which just cannot be truthful and cannot be trusted: I have in mind cases in which b utters a sentence which is contradictory; it is not clear to me how Lewis's theory can accommodate such usage of language, and it is interesting to see what happens in connection with (III.1) and (III.2) when such usage occurs. Suppose that $E_b p$ in (III.1) describes b's act of uttering a contradictory sentence — "it is raining and it is not raining", for example. Let q be that sentence, and suppose that (III.2) is true. It can then easily be shown that it is not logically possible for (III.3) to be true, for were it to be true then (III.6) would follow, but (III.6) is provably false wherever q is itself contradictory. a cannot believe that, according to the information available to b, it is both raining and not raining. This result seems to me entirely satisfactory — it is just what would be expected of such a situation; an audience cannot possibly believe that utterance to him of a contradictory sentence best meets his interest in being informed. However, all this does not preclude the possibility that b performs this speech act in Z with some purpose in mind, a purpose which he believes he might be able to achieve *just because* he thinks it will be clear to a that the utterance could not possibly be taken as non-deceiving in the above sense. Suppose, for example, that a believes that b is generally not one to perform such apparently pointless speech acts, and suppose that b is aware of this. Then b has good grounds for thinking that when he does utter this contradictory sentence, a will wonder why he did so, what his intention was; and then there may be sufficient background information available to a, about b and perhaps about other matters, for a to arrive at the correct explanation of why b uttered the contradictory sentence in the first place. For example, a might come up with the explanation that b intended to indicate, by uttering this sentence, that he was bored.

It is not difficult to construct all manner of scenarios, which are by no means far-fetched, in which a communicator performs an apparently pointless speech act in order thereby to produce some further effect on his audience. The point to emphasize here is that he may expect to achieve his effect in virtue of the fact that it will be clear to his audience that *because* the speech act he actually performs is apparently pointless they need to seek some explanation of why he performed it. The mutual belief of type (III.1) is being exploited to achieve some further end. Of course it may have been possible for b, the communicator, to produce his intended effect by some other means, and it may be that the audience misinterprets his intention, and comes up with the wrong explanation of why b did what he did. Nevertheless, we have here an outline sketch of one way in which mutual beliefs of type (III.1) can be exploited. Herein is an account of *one* way in which a communicator can say one thing and mean another. It is also clear, I hope, that not only contradictory utterances can serve such purposes; supposing that *b* did wish to indicate to *a* that he was bored, he might have chosen to perform instead any other apparently pointless speech act: perhaps he starts uttering banalities which have no connection whatever with the conversation then in progress, expecting that *a* will not then believe that *b*'s speech acts best meet his interest in being informed, and that *a* will look for some explanation of *why* the speech acts were performed.

What creates the possibility for the communicator to use a strategy of this sort is, essentially, the mutual belief of type (III.1). For, as we have seen, the structure of (III.1) is such that, given (III.2), *a* would believe that $V_b q$ were he to *trust* that *b*'s act was non-deceivingly performed.

A second type of trust was noted in passing in Chapter I. If *a* goes on, on the basis of (III.6), to form belief (III.7) he will be said to trust that *b* is reliably informed:

(III.7) $B_a q$.

Given the form here suggested for rules of information, it is clear that the outcome of a communication situation will be largely determined by the extent of trust, of the two types, on the part of the audience. I refer to the two types as "trust of type no-deceit" and "trust of type reliability", respectively.

Situations in which the distinction between these two types of trust is operative are commonplace; situations in which it is put to further use abound in counter-espionage. An espionage agent may be supplied with information which, unbeknown to him, is unreliable, but which he then supplies to *a*; suppose that the agent's source of information is *c*, that *c* knows that the agent will pass on the information to *a* and, further, that *a* knows both that the agent's information is unreliable and that it emanates from *c*; it may now happen that, although he does not trust that the agent's information is reliable, *a* nevertheless has good grounds for supposing that the agent's acts of transmitting information to him are non-deceivingly performed — and so *a* draws conclusions about what, according to the information available to the agent, is the case. On the basis of these conclusions, *a* may form a picture of what it is that *c* *wants* him (*a*) to believe, for he is aware that *c* channels information to him through the agent; and of course it may be very useful for *a* to find out what *c* wants him to believe.

It is easy to see that a further twist can occur here: suppose *c* finds out that a takes the information supplied through the agent not as true, but merely as an indication of what c wants him to think; then, at some suitably strategic moment, c might pass on true information through the agent to a, confident that a will then draw the conclusion that this information is just what he should not believe. A case rather like this one is cited in Goffman, 1970, p. 57.

So much, for the moment, for audience trust. Suppose again that (III.1) is true and that b knowingly brings about p in circumstances Z. Then b will be said to be *truthful relative to the information available to him* if (III.8) is true:

(III.8)　$V_b q$;

furthermore, b will be said to be *sincere* in his performance of the communication act if, when he performs it, (III.9) is true:

(III.9)　$B_b q$.

I next turn to a well-known philosophical puzzle to provide further illustration of some of the distinctions drawn in this section.

III.2. MOORE'S PARADOX OF SAYING AND DISBELIEVING

The puzzle Moore formulated is basically the following (see Hintikka, 1962, p. 64, for a list of relevant literature): the conjunction expressed by (III.10) is not inconsistent —

(III.10)　It is raining and I do not believe that it is raining

— and yet there is something very odd about that conjunction; any proposal for a solution to the puzzle has to explain the nature of that oddity.

The essence of Hintikka's formal diagnosis (*op. cit.*, Sections 4.5–4.7) is that, in *his* logic of belief, (III.11) and (III.12) are defensible, whereas (III.13) is indefensible:

(III.11)　$p \cdot {\sim} B_a p$
(III.12)　$B_b(p \cdot {\sim} B_a p)$
(III.13)　$B_a(p \cdot {\sim} B_a p)$.

Thus, as far as Hintikka's system is concerned, it may be the case both that it is raining and that a does not believe that it is raining, and it may be the case that b ($b \neq a$) believes both that it is raining and that a does not believe that it is raining; but, it is provably the case that a himself cannot believe both that it is raining and that he does not believe that it is raining.

In LC, (III.13) is not provably inconsistent: the possibility is left open that a's information about his own belief-state may be even as unreliable as in the situation described by (III.13); however, according to LC, (III.13) will be provably inconsistent in all those worlds which, relative to some given world, are ideal relative to a's interest in being informed — see above, pp. 67–68. So, although Hintikka's analysis of Moore's puzzle is not available to me, perhaps the oddity of (III.10) might be explained by saying that the truth of that sentence would constitute violation of an ideal which one ordinarily expects an agent's enquiring system to meet.

But I am not convinced that this really gets to the heart of the matter. Like Searle (1969, p. 65, fn. 1), I am inclined to think that the puzzle relates to certain features of the communication situation in which (III.10) is uttered; in particular, it is necessary to examine the roles of audience trust (of type reliability) and speaker's sincerity in that situation, in the light of the expectations an audience ordinarily has.

Let $E_b p$ in (III.1) describe b's act of uttering sentence (III.10), and let q be sentence (III.10). Suppose, further, that (III.2), (III.3) and, therefore, (III.6) also obtain, and that audience a now adopts an attitude of trust of type reliability with respect to b's speech act. Then (III.7) holds. Where r now stands for the sentence "it is raining", a's belief (III.7) may be represented by (III.14):

(III.14) $B_a(r \cdot \sim B_b r)$;

now suppose further that a believes that b is sincere in his performance of the speech act — in the sense earlier defined — in which case (III.15) is true:

(III.15) $B_a B_b(r \cdot \sim B_b r)$.

In virtue of uncontroversial properties of the logic of belief, (III.14) entails (III.16):

(III.16) $B_a r \cdot B_a \sim B_b r$

and (III.15) entails (III.17):

(III.17) $B_a B_b r \cdot B_a B_b \sim B_b r$.

The conjunction of (III.16) and (III.17) entails (III.18), and (III.18) expresses an inconsistency in virtue of the fact that (II.25) is provable in LC (see above, p. 56):

(III.18) $B_a B_b r \cdot B_a \sim B_b r$.

The root of the oddity in Moore's example thus resides in the fact that anyone who utters (III.10) *cannot* be supposed both to be telling the truth and to be sincere; the assumption of reliability requires the truth of the conjunction $r \cdot \sim B_b r$, but the assumption of sincerity requires the truth of $B_b(r \cdot \sim B_b r)$, which entails that $B_b r$. What happens in normal communication situations, by contrast, is that if a speaker is assumed to be saying something which is true then it is at least logically conceivable that he believes that what he is saying is true; and if the speaker is assumed to believe that what he is saying is true, then it should be at least logically conceivable that what he is saying *is* true.

This analysis of Moore's puzzle is very similar to that offered by Searle (*loc. cit.*), and is reached by taking up the viewpoint of an audience who tries to extract information from a speech act in which (III.10) is uttered. (In fairness to Hintikka, it should be pointed out that he does say that *one* way of explaining Moore's puzzle lies in the fact that (III.13) cannot be consistently conjoined with (III.11); (see Hintikka, 1962, pp. 70–71). It seems clear, however, that Hintikka's *preferred* solution turns on the indefensibility (in his system) of (III.13) itself.)

III.3. INFORMING AND ASSERTING

The previous two sections have concentrated largely on the process whereby an audience a may extract information from a signalling or linguistic act which he believes to have been performed. I have not as yet fully specified what it is for a communicator b to *inform* a that q by doing p in Z and, in particular, no definition has yet been given of what it means to say that b *asserts* that q by doing p in Z. This section shifts the focus of attention from the role of the audience to that of the communicator. I again confine the discussion to the kind of situation in which transmission of information from b to a is made possible by the fact that b and a have a mutual belief of type (III.1). And, for simplicity, I again consider the two-person situation.

Suppose that (III.1), (III.2), and (III.3) are all true. It may still fail to be the case that b is informing a that q, for the simple reason that a might be mistaken in his belief (III.2). Perhaps b has not in fact brought about p, or has not brought about p in circumstances Z.

What is it then for b to inform a that q by doing p in Z? The term "informing", just like the term "communicating", is very vague and covers a pretty broad spectrum of cases. Some stipulation is called for here. If it is supposed that (III.1), (III.2), and (III.3) all obtain, then I shall say that the broadest range of cases of which it is true to say that b informs a that q is obtained by adding the requirement that (III.19) be true:

(III.19) $E_b p \cdot Z$

— that is, the supposition is added that b actually does perform the act in circumstances Z. But it is not difficult to see that, within this broad range, many different possible types of communication situation remain. There now follows a description of some of them and, importantly, for some of the possible cases reference will need to be made to b's intentions, and for this purpose the modality Shall will be employed.

To make the description of the cases sound a little more realistic, suppose that $E_b p$ describes b's act of projecting his arm out of the right-hand side window of his car, that q describes the circumstance that b is about to turn his car to the right, and that the Z factor indicating contextual features describes the context as being one in which a and b are both using the highway, b being the driver of a car.

Against the background of (III.1), (III.2), (III.3), and (III.19) suppose now that:

	(i)	b is not aware of doing p; i.e. $\sim B_b E_b p$; perhaps b is drunk or being careless, or both;
or	(ii)	b is aware of doing p but did not intend to do it; i.e. $B_b E_b p \cdot \sim B_b$ Shall $E_b p$;
or	(iii)	b is aware of doing p but not aware of the fact that a saw him doing it; i.e. $B_b E_b p \cdot \sim B_b B_a E_b p$;
or	(iv)	b is aware of doing p but did not intend to get a to notice him doing it; i.e. $B_b E_b p \cdot \sim B_b(E_b p \rightarrow$ Shall $E_b B_a E_b p)$;
or	(v)	b is aware of doing p and intends to get a to notice him doing it; i.e. $B_b E_b p \cdot B_b(E_b p \rightarrow$ Shall $E_b B_a E_b p)$;
or	(vi)	like (v) but with the added feature that b intends to get a to believe that his act of bringing about p in Z best meets a's interest in being informed; i.e. add to (v): $B_b((E_b p \cdot Z) \rightarrow$ Shall $E_b B_a O_a(E_b p \cdot Z))$.

Here there are just six cases; each one of these six has at least two sub-cases, depending on whether or not q is in fact true. And it is easy to construct others besides these. Each of (i)–(vi) will be said to be a case of b's informing a that q by doing p in Z; this does not imply that a forms the belief that q on the basis of witnessing the signal – merely that a forms the belief (III.6). (For the example at hand, it is more than likely that a will in fact also believe that q *given that* he believes that $V_b q$, for he will generally have good grounds for supposing that b is reliably informed about what he (b) is going to do.)

It may be objected that the stipulation here made as to what counts as informing wrongly excludes many cases. It might be maintained that some of (i)–(vi), for example, would still be instances of informing even if (III.3) were not true. Case (v), it might be thought, is one in which b informs a that q (by doing p in Z) regardless of whether a trusts b to be non-deceiving. For b does intend to get a to notice his performance of the signalling act. I agree that the notion of informing is vague enough to create controversy over a case like this one. My inclination is to say that here we have an example in which b is perhaps trying to inform a but does not succeed; my stipulation is that a is not informed (and that, therefore, b does not inform a) until he forms the belief that $V_b q$.

It may be that those who would be inclined to classify this last case as one of genuine informing have another point in mind: perhaps they feel that the communicator's intentions provide the key to proper classification here and that (v) and (vi), but none of (i)–(iv), are cases of informing, regardless of whether (III.3) holds. I agree that classification along such lines might also be feasible. But what I have in mind is to use reference to communicator's intentions, not in defining the class of acts of informing, but in defining a sub-class of that class: acts of *asserting*. In the end it *may* be that little is gained one way or the other by adopting this pattern of classification rather than the other; my intuition is, anyway, that asserting is a *species* of informing – it is an act of informing which the communicator performs with certain intentions; all of the features mentioned in case (vi) are necessary for the successful performance of an act of asserting. Case (v) falls short because it does not specify that b intends a to trust that his act is non-deceiving; (all the other cases fall short because they do not even require that b intends a to notice that he has brought about p in Z). But why require that b intends a to trust his performance? The answer is that b's asserting that q involves his commitment to the truth of q – it may be said to constitute an undertaking to the effect that, relative to the information available to *b, q* is true; (*cf.* Searle, 1969, p. 66). If *b* is to intend that his act count as an undertaking to the effect that his information is that *q*, it is natural to require that he intends that his act be believed to be non-deceiving.

It may be thought that even case (vi) falls short of a set of necessary *and* sufficient conditions for the fully "felicitous" performance of an act of asserting. Suppose that *a* does not believe that *b* has the intentions specified in (vi); then, from his point of view, this does not count as an act of asserting. Or, suppose that *b* does not believe that *a* believes that he (*b*) has these intentions ... and so on. In the end, what is required here is that *a* and *b* *mutually* believe both that *b* intends his act to be observed by *a* and that *b* intends his performance to be trusted by *a*.

Note that this account of asserting leaves open the possibility that *b* asserts that *q* by doing *p* in *Z* but is insincere — he is not required to believe that *q*. And, as any reasonable account of asserting must, it leaves open the possibility that *b* is telling a lie — he might know that *q* is false. Furthermore, *b* may assert that *q* (to *a*) without intending to get *a* to believe that *q* and without intending to get *a* to believe that he (*b*) believes that *q*. (That asserting is compatible with the absence of these intentions seems to be suggested by Searle — see *loc. cit.* and his (1971), pp. 8 and 10.) I admit that if *a* does not think that *b* intends to get him to believe both that *q* and that he (*b*) believes that *q* then *a might* have some grounds for thinking that *b* did not intend his utterance-act to be taken as non-deceiving; but even if that is generally true it does not follow that *b* must intend to get *a* to believe that *q* and that he (*b*) believes that *q*; rather, he must intend to get *a* to believe that he (*b*) has those intentions.

The diagnosis proposed earlier of Moore's paradox of saying and disbelieving can now be extended in the light of the account of asserting. According to that account it is *possible* for *b* to assert (III.10); but it is clear that any attempt *b* makes to assert (III.10) is quite likely to be unsuccessful; for, if *a* realizes that he cannot both believe *b* to be sincere and trust that *b*'s speech-act is reliable, he has good grounds for not believing that the speech-act is non-deceiving. According to the account here given, if *a* does not believe that act to be non-deceiving it is not one of informing — and hence not one of asserting. So here then is another aspect of the oddity of the utterance of (III.10): not only would a trusting (type: non-deceit) audience be put in the strange position earlier described, it is also the case that the speaker would have good grounds for supposing that the utterance would not come off at all as an act of informing or asserting.

Yet, regardless of whether the utterance does in fact succeed as an instance of asserting or informing, it is clear that the means are available, in LC, for describing just what *is* essentially going on in an "abortive" communication situation of this sort.

III.4. TRUST OF TYPE NO-DECEIT, COMMUNICATORS' INTENTIONS AND "SAYING ONE THING AND MEANING ANOTHER"

I have distinguished between the meaning of the act and what the act is actually taken to be a sign of, or evidence of, (if anything), on a particular occasion of its performance; and I have distinguished between both of these and the notion of what b meant by (intended to do by) performing the act.

Suppose, again, that (III.1) and (III.2) are true, that a is correct in his belief (III.2) and that a and b are mutually aware that he has brought about p in Z. Both a and b believe that b's act means that q, regardless of whether either of them believes that b's performance is non-deceiving; *because b* is aware of what a takes the act to mean the possibility is created for b to make use of that act to achieve certain intended ends. Frequently his intention will be to assert that q — in which case he will intend a to believe that his performance *is* non-deceiving; and, maybe, he intends to assert that q in order to help try to fulfil a further intention to get a to believe that q; but this common intended usage of the act does not exhaust the possibilities open to b as communicator. He might, for example, make it patently clear to a that his performance is not, and is not intended to be, non-deceiving (in which case a will not take the act as a sign that, according to the information available to b, q is true), in order thereby to produce some effect on a's beliefs; and he might further expect that the production of this effect will be in part dependent upon a's belief about what the act means.

To illustrate this last possibility consider the following example: a and b are again road-users, this time both are driving vehicles; imagine that they have been caught for some time in a traffic-jam, crawling along at very low speed, with a driving behind b. Suppose that b wishes to inform a that he is getting pretty fed up with driving in the queue; of course there are various ways in which he might be able to do this, but what he does in fact is to put his right arm out of the right-hand window and wave it up and down several times, slowly and deliberately. b is aware that his act will be taken by a (and indeed by any other driver familiar with traffic signals) as meaning that he (b) is about to slow down. He expects, however, that a will appreciate that this is not a non-deceiving performance, since it is clear to him that b could hardly be travelling any more slowly than he is already. He expects, further, that *a* will seek some explanation of why he (*b*) gave the signal and he expects that the fact that *a* believes that the signalling act actually means "*b* is about to slow down" will itself play a role — that it will suggest to *a* that what *b* really *means by performing* the act has something to do with the speed at which they are travelling; *b* expects that *a*'s awareness of the meaning of the act will be instrumental in the production of his (*b*'s) intended effect.

It may well be that *b* fails to secure his intended effect, for he is asking a great deal of *a*'s capacities to interpret; but whether or not he succeeds is beside the point as regards the purpose of this example. It is by no means ridiculous to suppose that, by performing the signalling act, he led *a* to form a belief the content, topic or theme of which was suggested to *a* by his (*a*'s) awareness of the fact that the act meant "*b* is about to slow down". But if no distinction is made between what a signalling act means and what its performance on a particular occasion actually is a sign of, and between what a signalling act means and what the signaller meant by performing it, it is difficult to see how the possibility of this kind of communication can be explained.

As applied to *speech* acts the distinctions here made help to explain how it is possible for *b* to say one thing and mean another. Suppose that a verbal indicative signalling system is sufficiently complex in structure to be classifiable as a natural language. According to the analysis given in Chapter I, the performance of a verbal indicative signalling act is assigned the same meaning as is assigned to the sentence delivered in the performance of that act. But this of course does not preclude the further distinction between the meaning of the act and what the performer meant by performing the act. So *b* can say "It's cold here" and mean by saying that sentence that it is warm there. On my analysis the act performed and the sentence uttered mean that it is cold there (in the place where *b* is speaking); but *b* may intend, by performing that speech act, to produce in his audience the belief that it is warm; furthermore, he may expect that the fact that the audience is aware of what the sentence means will play a part in the production of his intended effect on their beliefs. The topic referred to by the sentence he actually utters is related to the topic about which he intends his audience to form some belief — the sentence concerns the temperature in the room; *b* will presumably make it clear to his audience that his performance of the speech act is not intended to be non-deceiving, expecting them then to seek some explanation of why he performed it, and expecting that their awareness of the fact that the topic of the sentence uttered was the temperature in the room will help guide them towards the correct interpretation of what he meant by performing the act.

As in the case of the "slowing-down signal" example, things may easily go wrong for b; he may be mistaken in thinking that a will see the connection between the meaning of what he says and what he meant by saying it. Whether or not b is successful will depend on a variety of factors, including, of course, how well b and a know one another, how familiar a is with the kinds of techniques b employs for suggesting one thing by saying another. But, in rough outline, the structure of the kind of communication situation here under consideration may be represented as follows:

(i)   (III.1) and (III.2) both hold;

(ii) b intends to bring it about that a believes that his performance is not non-deceiving, i.e.,
        B_b Shall $E_b B_a \sim O_a(E_b p \cdot Z)$;

(iii) b believes that if (III.1) and (III.2) hold and a believes that the act performed is not non-deceiving, then a will believe that b intends to produce in him the belief that r; i.e.
        $B_b(((\text{III.1}) \cdot (\text{III.2}) \cdot B_a \sim O_a(E_b p \cdot Z)) \to B_a B_b$ Shall $E_b B_a r)$;

(iv) b expects that the topic described by q in (III.1) will help in suggesting to a what it is that b intends to get a to believe.

In Section III.1 I mentioned examples of another kind of way in which a communicator may say one thing and mean another; in those cases the communicator expected that the audience's awareness of the meaning of the act performed/sentence uttered would lead him to believe that the utterance was not non-deceiving, and also expected that the audience would then seek some explanation, in terms of the communicator's intentions, of why the act was performed. But he did not expect that the meaning of the act performed/sentence uttered would itself suggest to the audience the topic about which he intended the audience to form some belief. So the mechanism which the communicator there expected to be operative in producing his intended effect on the audience seems to differ from that described above, with respect to clause (iv).

Although the description given in terms of (i)–(iv) above is but an outline sketch of the structure of that type of communication situation, it does nevertheless help one to see more clearly the manifold ways in which the attempt to say one thing and mean another may misfire. Consider, for example, clause (ii) in the case of b's saying "It's cold here" and meaning "It's warm here"; it may be that b expects a to see that his utterance is not non-deceiving in virtue of a's believing that it is indeed not cold, but warm, in the room; but then of course b might be quite mistaken in supposing that it is obvious to a that it is warm in the room. In fact in both literal and non-literal uses of language communicators often rely on the presupposition that they and their audience have certain shared perceptions regarding the nature of the surroundings or context in which the act of communication occurs. Where those presuppositions are themselves mistaken, misfires are likely to be unavoidable.

I do not claim to have here presented an exhaustive characterization of the ways in which a communicator may expect to be able to say one thing and mean another; (there may be various other ways, but my conjecture is that the framework of concepts here proposed will be adequate for the description of their main features.) My aim has been simply to indicate the roles of beliefs about meaning, of intentions, and of trust (of type no-deceit) in some instances of what might be called non-literal usage of language and signalling.

Lewis, 1969, p. 177, says this: "What sort of an action is it to give an interpretation to a sentence? Not something anyone can do just by putting his mind to it. I can't say "It's cold here" and mean "It's warm here" — at least, not without a little help from my friends". Nevertheless, I can say "It's cold here" and mean by saying it "It's warm here", in the sense that I intend by uttering the sentence to get my audience to believe that it is warm here, or that it is evident to me that it is warm here. There is no reason why I should not decide that that is the interpretation I intend the audience to put on my act. It may be unrealistic of me to suppose that I can in fact bring off the intended effect — and bringing it off *would* require a little help from my friends: for they must piece together the clues I give them concerning what my intention is; but they *might* recognize the mechanism that I am intending to exploit. Or it may even be that my intended effect is produced, but by means of some mechanism different from that which I expected to be operative — and therein lies another interesting possible complication to the often tortuous process whereby an audience interprets what the communicator means by what he does.

III.5. NON-DECEIVING PERFORMANCES AND THE IMPLEMENTATION OF RULES OF INFORMATION

Suppose again that (III.1) and (III.2) are true — and, further, that a is correct in his belief (III.2) (in which case (III.19) is true). What would then constitute reasonable grounds for a's forming the belief described by (III.3) — the belief that b's act best meets his (a's) interest in being informed, and is in that sense non-deceiving?

It is obvious that if a has independent evidence (evidence independent of b's communicative act) that $V_b q$, then he has good grounds for accepting b's act as non-deceivingly performed; but that kind of case is not interesting: for it is a case in which, as regards a's becoming informed about $V_b q$, b's communicative act would be redundant.

Earlier I insisted that b's performance means that q regardless of b's intentions in performing the act — and I tried to give some reasons showing why it is useful, for explanatory purposes, to insist on just that. However, ignoring now the uninteresting cases mentioned in the previous paragraph, the intentions b is thought to have in performing the act *are* likely to be among the factors which a considers in making up his mind whether b's performance is non-deceiving and — in consequence — a sign that, according to the information available to b, q is true. For, generally speaking, unless a believes that b intended his act to count as an *instance of implementation* of the rule of information (III.1), he will not believe that b's performance was non-deceiving.

There are cases which constitute exceptions to this last statement, but they are quite unrepresentative of the usual types of communication situation; under the influence of a drug, or hypnosis, or in his sleep, b might perform some linguistic act which a has good grounds for thinking is non-deceiving; perhaps b says something which, were it to be true, would tie in very well with other facts known by a; or maybe a has grounds for believing that b is under the influence of a drug which generally has the effect of making people report non-deceivingly on the information available to them. But in such cases it would of course be incorrect to say that b is intentionally implementing the rules of information concerned, for he is not acting intentionally at all. Perhaps a comparable kind of situation is the one which can arise when a person is subject to the stress of interrogation or cross-examination — when, as is sometimes said, he lets some remark which he did not intend to make "just slip out"; it can happen, in such situations, that the audience has reasonable grounds for supposing that what "slips out" is in fact a reliable indication of the information available to the speaker.

But if exceptions of this sort are ignored, then it may be said that it will be a necessary condition of a's believing that b's act (of doing p in circumstances Z) is non-deceivingly performed that a also believes that b intended his act to be an instance of implementation of the rule of information (III.1).

A necessary condition — but by no means sufficient, for at least the following two reasons: (i) b might intend to implement (III.1) in order to be able to say one thing yet mean another; his aim will not then be to get a to believe that the act he performs is non-deceiving — on the contrary, as I suggested above, his aim is likely to be that he wants a to see that his act is *not* non-deceivingly performed, in the hope that a will then discover the correct explanation of *why* it was performed; (ii) b might intend his act to be an instance of implementation of (III.1) and intend to be taken by a as performing non-deceivingly — and still, of course, a might have good grounds for mistrust: what a knows about the kind of person b is, and what he knows about b's own interests, are among the factors which might persuade a not to accept b's act as non-deceivingly performed, in those circumstances.

Beliefs about the communicator's intentions (in performing the communicative act) are thus just one of the factors which the audience should consider in deciding whether to accept a performance as non-deceiving.

The discussion in this and the previous two sections suggests that the following general characterization can be formulated of what it is for an act to instantiate a rule of information: b's bringing about p in circumstances Z is mutually believed by a and b to be an instance of implementation of rule of information (III.1) if and only if:

(i) (III.1) holds

and (ii) $B^*_{ab}(E_b p \cdot Z)$

and (iii) $B^*_{ab}(B_b \text{Shall } E_b B_a O_a(E_b p \cdot Z) \lor B_b \text{Shall } E_b B_a {\sim} O_a(E_b p \cdot Z))$.

Clause (iii) here says that a and b mutually believe that either b intends to get a to believe that his performance is non-deceiving or b intends to get a to believe that his performance is not non-deceiving. For the first disjunct b may be said to intend a *literal* implementation of the rule of information, and for the second a *non-literal* implementation.

The issues covered in this section are relevant to the assessment of Bennett's defence of the Gricean theory — see below, Section V.1.

CHAPTER IV

NON-INDICATIVES

IV.1. NON-INDICATIVES AND TRUTH CONDITIONS

Those who would want to insist that an account of sentence meaning in an indicative language logically presupposes certain facts about the intended usage of such language, or its intended function, are right *only* to the following extent, it seems to me: the functions which determine meanings of sentences determine *truth* conditions (i.e. fix *truth values* for sentences in possible worlds) *because* indicative language is required by its users to serve the function of enabling the transmission of information about what is or is not the case.

When a language is considered entirely in abstraction from its use — when it is considered *purely* as an abstract semantic system — it does not matter what values are assigned to its meaning-determining functions; they can be given whatever names we like (*cf.* Cresswell, 1974, p. 18, who suggests the names "Big Ben" and "Walter Scott"). But when an abstract semantic system is thought of as a model of a natural (indicative) language, it is clear that the two *truth* values provide the required interpretation of these values. *That* much can be granted, however, without undermining Lewis's distinction between the description of an abstract semantic system, or possible language, and the description of the conditions under which such a system is adopted as a language by some population.

However, it is usual to suppose that the function of enabling the transmission of factual information is but one of the central functions which a natural language is supposed to serve; for such a language also contains non-indicative sentences, which do not appear to serve the function of permitting a speaker to show, and a hearer to learn, how things stand in some state of affairs. Dominant in the category of non-indicative sentences are imperatives and interrogatives; I shall concentrate on the former, suggesting later that interrogatives are a sub-category of imperatives. I shall have little to say about other types of non-indicatives; if the theory works for indicatives, imperatives and interrogatives it is not likely then to be rejected on the grounds that it has difficulties over, say, greetings and exclamations. However, I think it will not have difficulties even there; for, viewed from one angle, my proposals will be that there are no non-indicative usages of languages (or signalling systems) at all.

It was suggested earlier that there really is no need to distinguish between the meaning of a sentence-type and the meaning of the act-type in which a token of that sentence-type is delivered, provided that the distinction is made between meaning, in this sense, and the notion of what the agent meant by delivering the sentence; and just as I have talked of the meaning of act-types in which sentences are delivered, so also have I talked of the meaning of signalling act-types. Likewise, what now follows concerning the meaning of imperatives applies equally to imperative sentence-types, act-types which involve delivering tokens of imperative sentence-types, and imperative signalling act-types.

The basic problem then, in considering the meaning of imperatives, is whether imperatives can be given meanings by being assigned truth conditions, since their essential function seems to be to get people to do things, rather than to transmit information.

The contrast suggested in that last clause is, I believe, profoundly misleading, for it tempts one to accept the view that imperatives achieve their function, when they do so, independently of the transmission of information. But how is it that an imperative is able to achieve its effect on an audience, of getting the audience to do something, if not by means of the transmission to the audience of some information? As soon as we are clear about what kind of information that is, in the case of imperatives, we have the means available for fixing their truth conditions.

Some would want to say that imperatives do not transmit information because they are not *about* anything — they do not say how things stand; and so they are thought to lack truth values. I will maintain, on the contrary, that it is just because imperatives are "about something" — and in virtue of what it is that they are about — that they can succeed in achieving the effect of getting the audience to whom they are addressed to do something. My proposal is that imperatives be treated as act-descriptions of a particular kind. If we confine attention, for the time being, to the most usual type of case, for which the imperative has a *source* and a *recipient* (audience), then my proposal amounts to this: imperatives are descriptions of acts (performed by the source) of creating what may be described as a *normative relation* between the source and the recipient. I shall say that an imperative signalling act which means that p is to be done, or an imperative sentence-type "Do p", or an act of delivering a token of that sentence type, is *true* if and only if the source brings it about that it shall be the case that the recipient brings it about that p. Thus, where b is source and a recipient, then the logical form of imperatives is of the type exemplified in (IV.1):

(IV.1) E_b Shall $E_a p$.

In brief, then, imperatives are about the creation of a certain type of interpersonal relation − a normative relation, in which some agent requires of some other agent that he perform some act. (There is no reason why we should not allow that, in many cases, either the source or recipient, or both, is not an individual agent but a group of agents; but consideration of the way in which group action relates to individual action is beyond the scope of this essay.) If source b delivers an imperative expecting *thereby* to get a to do p, then he expects a's awareness of his (b's) creation of a normative relation between him (b) and a to play a role in securing that effect; in other words, b expects that the information transmitted by the imperative will be instrumental, if not the only instrument, in producing the effect.

In terms of wffs of type (III.1), therefore, we can say what it is for an act of communication to have imperative meaning by specifying in greater detail the nature of the variable q. Consider, for example, (IV.2):

(IV.2) $B_{ab}^*(((E_b p \cdot Z) \cdot O_a(E_b p \cdot Z)) \rightarrow V_b E_b$ Shall $E_a q)$.

(IV.2) entails that a believes that any non-deceiving performance in circumstances Z of the act described by $E_b p$ is a sign that, according to the information available to b, b has created a normative relation between himself and a, to the effect that a is to bring it about that q. This, in turn, entails that, from a's point of view, b's bringing about p in circumstances Z *means* that b requires a to do q, or, more simply, taking for granted that a is recipient and b source, it means the same as the sentence "Do q".

There are various kinds of imperatives, and there are various kinds of factors which b might be relying on in order to secure the result that a normative relation *of a particular type* is established by his act of communication. For example, he might be relying on his authority over a, or (if this is different) his power over a, in order to create a normative relation of the commanding or ordering type. At the other extreme, b might be relying on the fact that a is in a position of power or authority vis-à-vis him (b), in order to create a normative relation of type begging/entreating. Between these two poles there are types of imperatives which seem to call for no special relation of power or authority between communicator and recipient, such as advising and requesting.

The formula given in the consequent of the conditional embedded in (IV.2) does not reflect these differences; it captures that part of the meaning of imperatives which is common to all types of imperatives. Either by means of the sentence uttered (if it is a linguistic act which b performs), or by some other means (e.g., b is pointing a gun at a, b is wearing the uniform of a superior officer, b is down on his knees in front of a), b will try to make it clear to a which, if any, special background factors, pertaining to the nature of their relationship, he is relying on in his attempt to secure the result that a normative relation of *such-and-such a type* is established by his act of communication. Thus the full specification of the truth conditions for some particular types of imperatives will involve reference to such background factors as well, and it is clear that, in specifying these truth conditions, this reference can be made in the indicator of contextual circumstances, Z. I return to this issue shortly, in considering the role of trust in imperative communication; obviously, it is relevant to the question of how an imperative can be false.

I next consider (IV.2) in the light of some of the notions which were introduced in Chapter III. According to the definition of *communicator's sincerity* there proposed, b is sincere in his performance, in circumstances Z, of the act described by $E_b p$ if, given (IV.2), (IV.3) is also true:

(IV.3) $B_b E_b$ Shall $E_a q$.

Supposing, as is reasonable, that (IV.4) is true:

(IV.4) $B_b(E_b p \rightarrow p)$,

(IV.3) entails (IV.5):

(IV.5) B_b Shall $E_a q$;

according to the readings earlier suggested, (IV.5) means that b expects a to do p (again, this is *not* an expectation of the predictive type, although it may also be true of b that he thinks that a will do q). This result is quite satisfactory: b is insincere if he tells a to open fire but does not expect of a the performance of the act of opening fire.

One way in which b's act of issuing an imperative could fail to be *non-deceiving* would, of course, arise if it were not an instance of implementation of the relevant rule of information; consider, for example, the general who, drunk and asleep in his boots, mumbles an "order" to retreat.

It is, however, possible for b's act of issuing an imperative to be an instance of implementation of the relevant rule of information and yet still fail to be non-deceiving. For b might be fully aware of the fact that he is not in a position to create a normative relation of the type which his audience takes him to be trying to create. He might, for instance, issue an imperative of the commanding or ordering type and yet know that he has no relation of power or authority vis-à-vis a; in such a case, a would be mistaken if he took the act to be a non-deceiving performance of an act of commanding or ordering. In this case, the imperative — which is meant to be an imperative of the commanding or ordering type — is false. This does not mean that it might nevertheless be true if considered as an imperative of, say, the requesting type. For any act of imperative signalling (verbal or non-verbal) will be of a *particular* type, and it must be judged true or false as an instance of that type.

It is, I think, the communicator who decides what type of imperative his imperative signalling act is — he determines what sort of imperative the act is meant to be taken as. It will thus be the communicator's intentions which here determine *which*, if any, background features, pertaining to the nature of his power relationship vis-à-vis his audience, are to figure in the truth conditions for the act he performs. (It would be a mistake to suppose that this last sentence represents a concession to the Gricean theory. *Cf.*, above, p. 33.)

One consequence of the above account is that it will also be possible for the audience to make a mistaken identification of the type of imperative being addressed to him. So, for example, an audience might wrongly identify an imperative as one of the command type, and then wrongly draw the conclusion that no normative relation has been established — on the (perhaps correct) grounds that no authority backed the imperative. One typical outcome of a situation of this sort is that the communicator tries to clarify his intentions, perhaps by adding a remark to the effect that he was merely *asking*, and not trying to *tell* the audience what to do.

The situation can also arise in which audience a is correct in judging the performance of an imperative signalling act of the commanding or ordering type to be non-deceiving, but in which the imperative is false. For suppose that b, the communicator, mistakenly believes that he does have a position of power in relation to a, and issues an imperative of the ordering type, intending a literal instance of implementation of the relevant rule of information; a would now be correct in supposing that, according to the information available to b, b has created a normative relation of the said type vis-à-vis a; that is, a would be correct in forming a belief of type (IV.6):

(IV.6) $B_a V_b E_b$ Shall $E_a q$.

Furthermore, a would also be justified in refusing to trust the act to be *reliable*, in this case, if he knew that b in fact lacked the power which he (b) assumed to be backing his imperative; for b has not in fact created a normative relation of the ordering type. Thus, in cases of this kind, a genuine distinction between the two types of trust is maintained.

Whenever an act of imperative signalling (verbal or non-verbal) is of a type which presupposes the existence of a special kind of power relation between communicator and recipient, it is not difficult to construct examples of the above kinds, in which the imperative is false.

For other types of imperatives, however, it is difficult to see how a non-deceiving performance could fail to be true. Suppose, for example, that both b and a are fully aware that no special power relation obtains between them, and that b says to a "I ask you to leave"; and suppose that a is correct in believing the utterance to be a literal implementation of the relevant rule of information; then a believes that, according to the information available to b, b has brought about a normative relation between himself and a, to the effect that a is to leave. How could a then refuse to trust that the communicative act was also reliable (in my sense)? How could he justify not accepting that the normative relation was in fact established? The point to note here is that b is *not* taken to be relying upon any particular backing for the imperative — as he would have been trying (unsuccessfully) to do if he had said, instead, "I order you to leave". So the mere non-deceiving performance of the act of saying to a "I ask you to leave" seems to be enough to guarantee that the sentence uttered is true. The distinction between the two types of trustworthiness seems to be inoperative for cases of this sort.

Such cases exhibit a further important characteristic: if the communicator intends that his act is to be a literal implementation of the relevant rule of information, that in itself is sufficient to guarantee that the act is non-deceiving. Thus, for example, if b says to a "I ask you to leave", and intends his speech act to be taken as a non-deceiving performance (which means, according to the account given in Section III.5, that he intends a literal implementation of the relevant rule of information), then that will in general be sufficient to ensure that the performance *is* non-deceiving and hence, for a case of this kind, reliable too; and that, in turn, implies that the sentence uttered is *true*. Thus we have here cases in which "saying makes it so", given that the communicator has an intention of the kind just mentioned. Furthermore, it would appear that, for such cases, if the speaker intends his utterance to be a non-literal implementation of the relevant rule of information – as, for example, when he is just joking – that will in general be sufficient to guarantee that the sentence he utters is *false*.

Perhaps another way of describing this characteristic of such cases would be as follows: if what the speaker means by performing his speech act may be identified with the meaning of the sentence he utters, then the sentence he utters is true.

It seems to me that the difference between asking and requesting, on the one hand, and ordering and commanding, on the other, should not be overestimated; mere non-deceiving performance by *b* of the act of uttering "I order you to leave" to *a* is not itself enough to establish the normative relation between them (vis-à-vis *a*'s leaving); but it *will* be enough if *b* does have power over *a*. Rather than drawing a sharp dividing line between the two categories of imperatives, it is, I think, preferable to describe the situation in the following way, in order to bring out the quite genuine similarities: normative relations between people are such that the non-deceiving performance of certain types of communicative acts can be sufficient to establish them; but, for some particular types of normative relations to be established by the performance of communicative acts it is necessary that a relation of power/authority of a certain sort already exists between communicator and audience; when it *does* exist, the non-deceiving performance of the appropriate act of communication will again be sufficient to establish the normative relation; and, in those cases where the power/authority relation does already exist, and the communicator knows that it does, if the communicator intends his performance to be a literal implementation of the relevant rule of information, then that performance will indeed *be* non-deceiving.

When communicative acts are viewed in terms of the role of the two types of audience trust, and in terms of the notion of an intended literal implementation of a rule of information, a new perspective emerges on the idea that some of them are "verifiable by their performance" and, correspondingly, that some sentences are "verifiable by their use". So perhaps a new way of approaching the concept of *performativity* is to be found here. Whether or not that conjecture is sound, it is clear that the account here proposed for imperatives bears some close similarities to recent work on performatives.

IV.2. PERFORMATIVES

Since the publication of Austin's work on performatives (see, especially,

Austin, 1962, 1963), the literature on the subject has become extensive; (see, for example, Åqvist, 1972; Danielsson, 1973; and Andersson, 1975).

It is not my intention to enter in detail into the discussion of the nature of performatives and performativity as such, nor to give detailed comparison of my proposals about imperatives with the analyses given, by these writers, of performatives. I merely want to point out that some of what they have said about performatives ties in well with what I have to say about imperatives. In particular, since Lemmon's 1962 paper, the idea has been current that the notion of *verifiability by use* might be employed in the definition of the class of performative sentence-types. Also, in Andersson (*op. cit.*, see, for example, pp. 44–45), there is the idea that speech acts in which performative sentences are used are employed to create certain *normative consequences*; this, again, might fit in well with my proposals about imperatives (although I suspect we would disagree with respect to ways in which normative elements are to be incorporated in the analysis of *asserting*). Finally, the proposals made in Sesonske (1965) may overlap in interesting ways with mine; he discusses utterances whose point is to alter the nature of the relation obtaining between the communicator and the audience. Although, according to *his* definition of performative utterances – which picks out a sub-class of the cases considered by Austin – imperatives in my sense would not be performatives, because imperatives alter what he calls *generative* relations rather than *formal* relations, his proposals are relevant to mine. In fact, I think that a good deal can be learned about non-indicatives in general by viewing them as devices used in communication to alter, establish or confirm relations of certain sorts between communicator and audience. I do not intend to try to assess the value of Sesonske's proposals about the appropriate classification of these relations; but I do think that normative relations will have to figure prominently in any adequate classification of them.

Austin was preoccupied with the *other* things speakers can do with language – apart from saying that such-and-such is the case. He tried to work out a distinction between performatives and constatives, but no matter how hard he tried it seemed that some constatives (of the type "I assert that ...", "I state that ...", "I declare that ..." and so on) would always turn out to be members of the class of performatives. This apparent failure set him off in hot pursuit of illocutionarity and resulted in a theory which, in my opinion, has never been of much value in the analysis of speech and language because its basic terms (locutionary, illocutionary and perlocutionary act) have never been sufficiently clearly defined. The confusion was increased by his attempt to maintain a particular position with respect to the relative roles of intention and convention in communication; both his argument and that in Strawson (1964) suffer from the fact that they are conducted in the total absence of any attempt to say precisely what a convention is. An account of that notion was lacking until the appearance of Lewis (1969).

Despite the fact that the performative/constative dichotomy could not be maintained in the way Austin wanted, it remains possible that the class of performatives is of crucial importance in understanding the nature of non-indicative language use. It may well turn out that the class of performatives, properly defined, will contain all non-indicatives but only some indicatives. Without entering into the details of the definitional problem, let me say that my feeling is that Lemmon's basic move was the right one, employing the notion of verifiability by use; and it will yield, I suspect, a more interesting distinction than that between performative and constative, or that between indicative and non-indicative. It will distinguish, in the class of sentences/ signalling acts, between those which are verifiable by their delivery/performance and those which are not; and my conjecture is that all non-indicatives will fall in the former category, and will do so because their use is, generally, to establish or alter certain types of interpersonal relations — for it just is the case that some types of interpersonal relations may be established or transformed by the mere utterance of a string of words, or by the mere production of a non-verbal signal, in the appropriate circumstances, given that these acts are non-deceivingly performed, in my sense.

These speculations about the potential usefulness of the concept of performativity will not be pursued further here. I do not rest my case for the proposed analysis of imperatives on the claim that they are performatives, but on the contention that if the logical form of imperatives is viewed in the way suggested, then the resultant logic of imperative inference is intuitively acceptable; a number of examples of imperative inferences are examined in the next section, in an attempt to defend this contention.

Nevertheless, since I do believe that an adequate definition of the class of performatives will have to include imperatives in that class, then I am open to an objection which itself turns on the issue with which this chapter began. Austin maintained that a simple imperative sentence such as "Open the door" is equivalent to a counterpart performative of the type "I request you to open the door", or "I order you to open the door", for example; and he used that supposed equivalence in one of his arguments designed to show that performatives lack truth values (see Austin, 1963, pp. 40–41). Taking it for granted that the imperative lacked a truth value, he used its alleged equivalence to the counterpart performative to show that it too lacked a truth value. However, if independent arguments can be supplied to support the idea that Austin was mistaken, and that performatives do indeed have truth values, then Austin's position can be turned around, and used as a means of defending the claim that imperatives have truth values. (Turning Austin's argument on its head in this way might also provide a means of giving it a body, since an account now becomes available of the notion of "equivalence" involved — Austin, so far as I am aware, did not offer an account of it.)

I have reviewed elsewhere some arguments for accepting that performatives do have truth values (Jones, 1976, and *cf.* Lewis, 1972, p. 210).

The idea of treating sentences in grammatically non-indicative moods as performatives has been employed in transformational generative grammar (see, e.g., Ross, 1970; Lakoff, 1972; Lewis, 1972). Whether one accepts that the successful use of the performative analysis for *that* purpose lends support to the claim that, for example, imperatives are *semantically* equivalent to their syntactic performative counterparts depends on one's attitude to the basic hypothesis of generative semantics (*cf.* Jones, 1976).

I think that the discussion to follow in the next section, concerning the logic of inferences involving imperatives, itself lends support to the performative paraphrase thesis, assuming that it is reasonable to suppose that the logical form of, e.g., "I request you to do *p*" is essentially the same as (IV.1), where the first person is replaced by *b* and the second person is replaced by *a*.

IV.3. SKETCH FOR A LOGIC OF IMPERATIVE INFERENCE

The aim in this section is to examine how the proposal made concerning the logical form of imperatives may be applied to the analysis of some arguments involving imperatives. I also raise some criticisms of a different approach to the logic of imperatives which has been favoured by a number of contributors to this field. (See, for example, Espersen, 1967; Rescher, 1966; Sosa, 1966a and b; Hofstadter and McKinsey, 1939). These logicians have adopted what I shall call the *satisfaction theory*, according to which an imperative is not assigned a truth value, but may be given the value *satisfied* or *not-satisfied* (fulfilled/non-fulfilled, obeyed/non-obeyed; Rescher actually prefers the labels *terminated/not-terminated*).

In Lewis (1972) the treatment offered of non-indicatives adopts the performative paraphrase approach, as has already been mentioned. However, in Lewis (1969) imperatives are analysed in conformity with the satisfaction theory, (see p. 150), despite the fact that he extends the application of the labels "true" and "false" to imperatives. He defends the extended use of these terms on the ground that it points to a symmetry between imperatives and indicatives: ". . . the signal either asserts or commands a certain state of affairs to hold, and is true if that state of affairs does hold." (*loc. cit.*; note that his treatment of imperatives in these terms is not confined to non-verbal imperative signalling – see also pp. 184–6.)

Suppose the imperative "Do p" is represented by: $!p$. Then one way to bring out the oddity of the approach taken by Lewis and the other satisfaction theorists is to point out that they would seem to be committed to the view that (IV.7) is a *valid* wff

(IV.7) $!p \rightarrow p$.

According to Lewis's extended usage of the truth values, and according to the way he assigns them to imperatives, whenever the antecedent of (IV.7) is true the consequent is also true. The counterpart of (IV.7) was indeed valid in Hofstadter and McKinsey's logic (*op. cit.*). Later satisfaction-theorists do not validate (IV.7), but it is difficult to see how they can consistently apply the values they adopt and yet not validate that wff. One *wants* to be able to say, concerning (IV.7), that the fact that the imperative $!p$ is issued or in force does not imply that it is satisfied; but this kind of comment is out of order for a satisfaction theorist, unless he from time to time conveniently slips away from satisfaction values and uses instead different values such as "issued"/"not issued", "in force"/"not in force". Compare the satisfaction-theorists' attitudes towards wffs (IV.7) and (IV.8):

(IV.8) $\sim(!p \cdot !\sim p)$;

concerning (IV.8) he would be happy to apply satisfaction-values; (IV.8) must be valid because, at one moment of time, an agent could not possibly satisfy both $!p$ and $!\sim p$. But it is precisely this type of reasoning which is *not* applicable to (IV.7), if the invalidity of (IV.7) is to be upheld, for an agent could not possibly satisfy $!p$ without bringing it about that p is true.

In the end, I think, a satisfaction-logic of imperatives can be seen really to be a disguised logic of act-descriptions which shows what other act-descriptions must be true if some given set of act-descriptions is supposed true.

It may be objected that satisfaction-theorists can avoid being committed to accepting (IV.7) as valid by imposing a constraint of the following sort on the definition of validity: an indicative is logically deducible from some set P of premises only if it is deducible from the indicative members of P alone.

Such a constraint may well be justified, but if we ask *why*, a satisfaction-theorist will not be able to tell us; for the proper explanation will have to appeal to just those aspects of the differences in meaning between indicatives and imperatives which his semantical values fail to capture.

In terms of my own proposals, (IV.7) takes the form of (IV.9):

(IV.9) E_b Shall $E_a p \rightarrow E_a p$,

and (IV.9) is of course not a theorem of LC; b may issue the imperative and a may adopt an attitude of trust of type no-deceit and an attitude of trust of type reliability to b's performance — and yet a might still fail to perform the act required of him. This is just how it should be.

The fact that (IV.8) *must* be a theorem in the satisfaction logic poses further problems. Agreed, an agent cannot carry out p and not-p at the same time, but does that mean that the conjunction of the imperatives !p and !$\sim p$ is logically false? Might not the source of the imperative be sufficiently irrational and unreasonable to issue conflicting imperatives? Is not (IV.8) a logical truth only if we assume that the source is rational to some degree? Is it not true to say that (IV.8) represents not so much a logical truth as a rationality assumption? If one feels, as I do, that these questions reflect genuine doubts about the status of (IV.8), the best policy seems to be to try to construct the logic of imperatives first of all in such a way that (IV.8) is not a theorem, and then compare that logic with an extension of it achieved by imposing the further constraint required to validate (IV.8). In that way one can systematically investigate just what the consequences are of the assumption that an imperative of the form (!$p \cdot$!$\sim p$) is not logically possible. But, obviously, this policy is not open to the satisfaction-theorist. For him there can be no question as to the validity of (IV.8).

The conditions *presently* governing LC do validate (IV.10):

(IV.10) $\sim(E_b$ Shall $E_a p \cdot E_b$ Shall $\sim E_a p)$

which is the counterpart in LC to (IV.8). However, if the condition (Q.Ser) on R(Shall) is dropped then (IV.10) ceases to be a theorem — and such a move can be motivated by appeal to considerations of the type just raised. Another way of expressing the consequence of dropping (Q.Ser) from (R.Shall) is to point to the fact that (II.24) then ceases to be a theorem. Wherever relevant, I will point out the role which (Q.Ser) might have played in the examples which follow.

One difficulty confronting a logic of imperatives is that of deciding on the correct form to choose for conditionals. Consider the sentence: "If it is raining, close the window" where b is source and a recipient. One way of tackling the problem is to start from the (surely correct) intuition that (IV.11) is a valid inference; given that the correct logical forms of second premise and conclusion are known, the range of possible formalizations of the first premise is then limited by the requirement that the result be a valid argument form:

(IV.11) (i)   If it is raining, close the window: ?
         (ii) It is raining: p
therefore (iii) Close the window: E_b Shall $E_a q$.

If (i) took the form:

$$p \rightarrow E_b \text{ Shall } E_a q$$

then the argument would be valid. But this formalization is unsatisfactory, for it says that b's creating the normative relation vis-à-vis a that a shall do q is conditional on the truth of p; this form is too weak, for it fails to capture the idea, which I think is implicit in (i), that the fact that b's creating this normative relation is conditional on p is itself something brought about by b. It does not just happen to be the case that b's creating the normative relation is conditional on p ... that is itself something which b sees to. Thus I propose the following as the form of (IV.11) (i):

$$E_b(p \rightarrow E_b \text{ Shall } E_a q).$$

It might be thought that there is no need to repeat the reference to b's agency in the consequent, and that, instead of the above, the following form could be used:

$$E_b(p \rightarrow \text{ Shall } E_a q).$$

But then the inference goes through only if (ii) is replaced by $E_b p$, which is odd, for b's creation of the normative relation is not supposed to be conditional on his *making* it rain. If we keep (ii) as it was we can, however, deduce Shall $E_a q$, which says that it shall be the case that, or that it is required of a that, he closes the window. I reject this proposal because I want reference to the source of the imperative to be carried through. If the conditional imperative emanates from the source b, then, if p is true, the imperative (iii) *also* emanates from source b and the logic should reflect this. And any attempt to argue that Shall $E_a q$ is, in fact, the correct logical form of "Close the window" should be rejected; for imperatives are not merely descriptions of what is required of some agent — they are not merely descriptions of norms to which an agent is subject — they are descriptions of the creation of normative relations between agents.

To see the proposal for conditional imperatives further applied, consider (IV.12), borrowed from Lemmon (1965):

(IV.12) (i)   If he comes, leave the files open.
        (ii) Do not leave the files open.
therefore (iii) He does not come.

This inference may be represented formally in LC as:

    (i) $E_b(p \rightarrow E_b \text{ Shall } E_a q)$
    (ii) $E_b \text{ Shall } \sim E_a q$
therefore (iii) $\sim p$

Castañeda (1960) accepts (IV.12) as valid and takes it to be a counter-example to Hare's claim that no indicative conclusion can be validly drawn from a set of premises which cannot be drawn from the indicatives among them alone. Castañeda thinks that if secretary a were given instructions (i) and (ii) she could infer that the person will not come; but, surely, she can make this inference only on the assumption that her boss, b, is being rational and reasonable and that he will not put her in the position in which, no matter what she does, she fails to meet some expectation he has of her. It is more likely, as Lemmon points out, that she will *hope* the other person does not come, or that she will conclude that her boss does not *think* that he will come. What is interesting here, from the point of view of LC, is that the relevance of consideration of the source's rationality is brought out *by* the logic, in as much as (IV.12) can be shown to be valid only on the assumption that (Q.Ser) does hold for R(Shall). In the absence of (Q.Ser), all that can be shown is that, if the person does come, the secretary's actions cannot fail to fall short of the normatively ideal. It follows, of course, that (IV.12) is going to be valid for the satisfaction-theorists, and so constitutes a further problem for them.

The formalization of disjunctive imperatives has been notoriously problematic. Any adequate treatment of them must meet the puzzle raised in Ross (1944) and now generally referred to as "Ross's Paradox". Disjunctive imperatives must not be symbolized in such a way as to validate the inference of "Do p or q" from "Do p". The basis of the solution here proposed has been given by Pörn (see the references in Section II.3, where a hint was

already given as to the way in which this puzzle can be dealt with) and
may be briefly described as follows: the point is that (R1) fails to hold for
the action logic, so no matter which of (i)–(iii) below we take as the logical
form of "Do p or q", it will not be deducible from (IV.1):

(i) $E_b(\text{Shall } E_a p \vee \text{Shall } E_a q)$
(ii) $E_b \text{ Shall } (E_a p \vee E_a q)$
(iii) $E_b \text{ Shall } E_a(p \vee q)$.

Of course it may be objected that (IV.13) is a theorem of LC:

(IV.13) $E_b \text{ Shall } E_a p \rightarrow \text{Shall } (E_a p \vee E_a q)$

since the antecedent entails Shall $E_a p$ and (R1) holds for Shall. But why
should this be taken to be an objection? The consequent here is *not* the
logical form of "Do p or q". But the question remains as to whether or
not (R1) should hold for the modality Shall; for example, if p is normatively
ideal, must it then follow that the disjunction of p and q is normatively
ideal? If the decision is that (R1) should not hold for Shall, then obviously
the possibility is open for modifying the logic of Shall along similar lines to
those employed for the correction of the action logic; one would then require
that whatever is normatively ideal in w is false in some world accessible to
w, but of course an account then has to be offered of how that new accessibility relation is to be understood intuitively. (In a forthcoming paper,
Pörn and I hope to formulate the details of an approach of roughly this
kind, applied to the analysis of deontic logic.)

Finally, I consider Chisholm's contrary-to-duty imperative paradox
(Chisholm, 1963). According to standard treatments of (monadic) deontic
or imperative logic (for which the semantics were basically analogous to
those for T, with seriality of the accessibility relation replacing reflexivity),
the following set (IV.14) of sentences, formalized as in (IV.14'), was provably
inconsistent:

(IV.14)   (i)   Go to the assistance of your neighbours;
          (ii)   If you go, tell them you are coming;
          (iii) If you don't go, don't tell them you're coming;
          (iv)   You do not go.
(IV.14') (i) $!p$
          (ii) $!(p \rightarrow q)$
          (iii) $\sim p \rightarrow !\sim q$
          (iv) $\sim p$

The inconsistency can be removed by either rewriting (IV.14′) (ii) as $p \to !q$ or rewriting (IV.14′) (iii) as $!(\sim p \to \sim q)$. The trouble is, however, that the members of (IV.14) appear to be not only mutually consistent but also logically independent of one another; if (IV.14′) (ii) is rewritten in the way just suggested it is entailed by (iv) (by the Law of Addition) and if (IV.14′) (iii) is rewritten in the way suggested it is entailed by (i), since Ross's paradox also holds for standard imperative logic. Two observations are in order here: first, there appears to be no good reason for assigning distinct logical forms to the conditional imperatives (IV.14) (ii) and (iii); second, if Ross's paradox is solved there will be a way of symbolizing this set of sentences so that it is consistent, its members are logically independent of one another and its two conditional imperatives are given the same kind of logical form. The set (IV.14*) fits the bill:

(IV.14*)　(i)　E_b Shall $E_a p$
　　　　　(ii)　$E_b(E_a p \to E_b$ Shall $E_a q)$
　　　　　(iii)　$E_b(\sim E_a p \to E_b$ Shall $\sim E_a q)$
　　　　　(iv)　$\sim E_a p$

As here presented the solution does not immediately trade on the solution earlier given to Ross's paradox. Nevertheless the failure of (R1) for the logic of action, which provided the basis for the solution to Ross's paradox, is safeguarding the set (IV.14*) from a possible line of objection: for suppose that (iv) were not the sentence "You do not go" but the sentence "I bring it about that you don't go"; then the set should still be logically consistent (despite the oddity of b's giving an imperative to a which he prevents him from fulfilling − that would be an unreasonable but not logically impossible thing for b to do) *and* its members should still be logically independent of one another; (IV.14*) (iv) would now take the form $E_b \sim E_a p$ and this *would* entail (IV.14*) (ii) were it not for the fact that (R1) fails to hold for the action logic. The solution here proposed lends further support to the claims earlier made about the logical form of conditional imperatives and keeps open the possibility that there is no need to resort to the construction of dyadic modalities in the analysis of such conditionals.

　　Here ends this brief outline sketch of the logic of imperative inferences; much more could be said − for example, concerning imperative inferences involving quantifiers (see MacKay, 1969; Clarke, 1970). But hopefully enough ground has been covered in this section to lend support to my proposals concerning the semantics of imperatives and to show that these proposals are preferable to at least one other type of approach to imperatives — the satisfaction theory.

IV.4. OTHER TYPES OF NON-INDICATIVES

The idea, which I here adopt, that interrogatives can be treated as a species of imperatives is by no means new. It is employed in Åqvist (1965) and Lewis (1969), for example. It is natural to treat interrogatives as requests for a specific type of action on the part of the audience, i.e., as requests that the audience supply information. Interrogative sentence-types, act-types of delivering tokens of them, and interrogative signalling act-types will be said to be true if and only if the source creates a normative relation vis-à-vis the recipient, to the effect that the latter is to supply information. Consider, for example, (IV.15):

(IV.15) $\quad B^{*}_{ab}(((E_bp \cdot Z) \cdot O_a(E_bp \cdot Z)) \rightarrow$
$\qquad V_bE_b \text{ Shall } E_a(K_bV_aq \vee K_bV_a{\sim}q));$

suppose that E_bp here describes b's act of delivering the sentence "Is Norway in Sweden?"; then q stands for the sentence "Norway is in Sweden"; b's question requires of a that a brings it about either that b knows that, according to the information available to a, Norway is in Sweden, or that b knows that, according to the information available to a, Norway is not in Sweden. It does not matter whether the question is given in the context of an examination: if it is, then — ideally at any rate — b already knows the answer; but whether or not b does already know the answer, what he wants to find out about is what is the case according to the information available to a. It might be objected that, where b *is* ignorant of the answer, what he wants to know is whether q is true, and not merely whether q is true according to the information available to a; but, by asking a, all that b can expect to get, obviously, is a's information on the matter; generally, if b is ignorant of the answer, he will of course not ask a unless he thinks that a is reliably informed on the matter.

What holds for imperatives of the requesting type generally, also holds for interrogatives: once a trusts b's communicative act to be non-deceiving he also trusts it to be reliable. (That is, the grounds a might have for not trusting the act to be reliable are likely also to be grounds for not trusting the act to be non-deceiving.) So although, like all other types of imperatives, interrogatives *can* be false, they share with requests the property that if the audience takes the communicator's performance to be non-deceiving he will usually also have to take the performance to be reliable; generally, the non-deceiving use of an interrogative makes the interrogative true.

The meaning of an interrogative may be exploited by its source in order to produce in the recipient some effect other than the belief that he is being asked a question. Consider again the example above, where b says to a "Is Norway in Sweden?"; on a particular occasion of the use of that sentence it may be perfectly obvious to both b and a that his performance of the speech act is not non-deceiving, in my sense, and so a does not form the belief that an act of creating a normative relation of the interrogative type has occurred. For b, knowing that a is a patriotic Norwegian, wishes to insult a — that is what b intends to do by uttering the sentence, that is what he means by uttering the sentence; b also expects to be able to produce this effect (of insulting a) in virtue of a's awareness of what the sentence uttered means. Here again we have an example of saying one thing and meaning another, and here again we see the advantage and explanatory value of keeping a sharp distinction between the meaning of the sentence and what the communicator meant by uttering it.

So far I have considered only one basic type of interrogative — what might be called the *Yes-No* interrogative. To provide truth conditions for such interrogatives as: "Where is Norway?", "How long will the Norwegian oil last?", "When did you visit Norway?", "What is that mountainous country to the west of Sweden?", a different specification (in each case) will be required of the formula which occurs to the right of the right-most action operator in (IV.15); no detailed proposals will be offered here, but it does seem reasonable to suppose that quantifiers ranging over the appropriate domains, together with the modalities K_a and V_a, will be needed.

Nor will the issue here be discussed as to how the formal model might need to be enriched in order to describe the dynamics of a question-answer sequence; the "statics" of the situation of both questioner and respondent may be described in the ways here indicated — if I am right. But it would seem that other formal devices — perhaps from games theory and cybernetics — are necessary to capture other aspects of the process which occurs when people question and answer.

It may be said, quite rightly, that there are cases in which a communicator asks a question, is perfectly sincere (in my sense) in his performance, and yet does not expect any answer. Sometimes questions are just raised for consideration, no answer being expected; for such cases I think it is still appropriate to talk in terms of the creation of normative relations (in terms of structures of the type E_b Shall E_a ...) but not to require that what the audience shall do is to provide an answer; what the audience is required to do is just to consider the matter raised by the question.

This suggests that the specification of the truth conditions for interrogatives should be broadened, to allow that what is required of the recipient is *either* that he supplies information to the questioner *or* that he simply considers the matter raised in the question; it seems not unreasonable to propose that what *a* is being asked to do, when he is asked by *b* to consider whether *q* is true, is to inform *himself* about the truth value of *q*. If that proposal is accepted, then the difference between the two disjuncts, in the formulation of the truth conditions for interrogatives, amounts to no more than a specification of the agent *to whom* information is to be supplied: the questioner or the recipient of the question.

On any particular occasion of utterance of an interrogative it will be the speaker's intentions which determine to whom it is that the information is to be supplied; when *b* puts some question or another to *a*, it will be in virtue of *a*'s knowledge of what the utterance means that he (*a*) also knows that *b*'s intention in making the utterance is the factor which determines to whom the information is to be supplied. The truth conditions of the utterance leave open for the speaker the opportunity either to use the utterance in order to try to get information for himself, or to use it to get the recipient merely to consider the matter. The point here seems to be parallel to one which arises in the proper analysis of the indexical "this": the *meaning* of that term is such that it enables a speaker to use the term to refer to or indicate whatever it is that he *intends* to refer to or indicate (*cf.* above, p. 33).

One might wonder how the account of interrogatives is to accommodate the following (very common) kind of case: *b* says to *a* "Would you be so kind as to open the door?"; it would ordinarily be quite inappropriate for *a* to answer by saying "Yes, my kindness does extend that far", for he is being asked to open the door rather than to comment on the extent of his kindness. I think my account can cope with this type of case quite easily, for (IV.15) is in fact neutral as regards which *means* are to be employed by the recipient for supplying the information requested; usually it is expected that the recipient is to supply the information verbally, but in the present kind of case the expectation is, normally, that *a*'s response will be action of a sort other than speaking. But what *a* does (or refrains from doing, as the case may be) still represents an answer to *b*'s question. It will ordinarily be features of context which indicate which mode of response the recipient of the question is to employ, but it is clear that the phrasing of the question itself may also play a role, as it does in the above example; the "would you be so kind as . . . ?" locution is almost always used to get the recipient to *show* his kindness, rather than to *comment* upon it.

I have considered certain types of imperatives, including interrogatives; are there not other non-indicatives?

It might be thought that there are imperatives which are undirected, in the sense that they are not addressed to any agent or group of agents; consider, for example, "Let there be light", "Let there be many sunny days this summer". What are their truth conditions? In keeping with the earlier proposals it might be suggested that these sentences describe acts of creating normative relations with states of affairs, and that these sentences therefore take the form: E_b Shall p. I agree absolutely with anyone who suggests that the idea of creating a normative relation with a state of affairs is a ridiculous one — for there is indeed something ridiculous in b's requiring of the world that it has such-and-such properties, *unless* b believes that some agency or other can produce those properties. But if we do suppose that there are imperatives which are totally undirected — not even directed to some unspecified agent — then their logical form is represented as given above. Alternatively, if it be granted that there must at least be some unspecified recipient, then the form should be: E_b Shall $(\exists x)E_x p$. I am inclined to think that, for genuine imperatives, there must be an act-description appearing immediately to the right of the Shall modality; the act-description may be relativized to the same agent as the one who issued the imperative: if and when God said "Let there be light" he certainly had in mind to perform the task himself. But if, as perhaps in the case of "Let there be many sunny days this summer", there is no implicit reference to any agency which is required to perform the act then it seems to me that we do not have a genuine impera-tive at all, but rather an expression of what, from the point of view of the speaker, would be optimal in the deontic rather than normative sense. I suspect, then, that the correct analysis of this sentence involves not Shall, but a deontic modality. Finally, let me also say here that I cannot make any sense of the notion of a *sourceless* imperative.

What of greetings and exclamations? A greeting is an act of creating a certain type of relation; if b says to a "Hallo", then the act performed is true if b does thereby acknowledge a's presence and false otherwise. Again it does not matter at all that b's act will generally be true if non-deceivingly performed; a performative type of analysis fits well here — this is an act verifiable by its performance; that type of relation which b enters into vis-à-vis a when b acknowledges a's presence is just the type of relation which can be established by the mere utterance of a word, or the mere raising of a hand or nod of the head. Performances which are not non-deceiving can occur — e.g. *b* says "Hallo" without realising that he is saying it. No harm is done by maintaining that, in such a case, the act performed is false.

One example of an exclamation, borrowed from Lewis, 1972, p. 209: "Hurrah for Porky"; *b*'s utterance of this sentence is true if he does cheer Porky (applaud Porky) and false otherwise; the sentence is verifiable by its use — mere (non-deceiving) utterance of it generally makes it true.

IV.5. NON-INDICATIVE USAGE OF INDICATIVES

It may be pointed out, by way of possible objection to the treatment offered for interrogatives, that it overlooks the fact that most, if not all, sentences in the grammatical indicative in English will function as interrogatives if they are uttered with the appropriate intonation contour.

My inclination is to cope with this fact by means of the distinction between what an utterance means and what a communicator means by delivering it; for example, if *b* utters the sentence "He has already left" with the characteristic rising intonation of an interrogative, then he can be confident that *a* will not take the performance as non-deceiving — i.e., that *a* will not draw the conclusion that, according to the information available to *b*, the contextually indicated third party has already left; the characteristic interrogative intonation contour is a quite reliable indicator, as far as the utterance of grammatically indicative sentences is concerned, of non-literal (i.e., not non-deceiving) implementation of the rule of information concerned. And because the usual function of that intonation contour is so well established among English-speakers, a communicator who employs it in the utterance of a grammatical indicative which means that *q* can be confident that his audience assumes that his purpose is to ask whether *q* is the case; (note again here that *b* makes use of the meaning of the sentence in conveying to his audience what he means by uttering it: the meaning of the sentence indicates to the audience what it is that *b* is asking about).

The distinction between the meaning of an utterance and what the communicator means by uttering it is also relevant to understanding the following kind of example: a mother says to her child "Your dinner is on the table", meaning thereby to issue an imperative to the child "Come to the table". Here, as in many other cases of saying one thing and meaning another, the mother expects the meaning of the sentence uttered to be instrumental in producing her intended effect. The sentence and (in my terms) the act performed mean that the child's dinner is on the table; the mother expects that the child will infer, from the fact that he is told that his dinner is on the table, that he is required to come to the table; the mother's expectation is reasonable because (but not *only* because) she knows that the child is aware of what the sentence means; it is unlikely that she could have reasonably expected to produce her intended effect by uttering instead a sentence the meaning of which did not suggest to the child that his food was ready. Unlikely, but not impossible: she might have said instead: "You know how often you have been disobedient lately". The child, understanding the meaning of what is said, wonders why it was said, looks up, sees the food on the table and then gets the point, the intention behind, the mother's utterance.

In cases of these sorts we have non-deceiving performance of an act of delivering an indicative — but the communicator's primary intention is not to say that such-and-such is the case, but to create a normative relation with a view to producing action from the audience.

Finally, it may be objected that the argument in these last two chapters has the consequence that a communicator can assert an imperative or assert an interrogative. Indeed, anyone who does not see that this is a consequence of my position has not understood it. But I do not take it to be an objection at all. For I have been trying to show that all communicative acts are acts of transmitting information and that, strictly speaking, there are no *non*-indicative uses of communication at all. But, despite that, I have also tried to point to interesting (and genuine) differences between what are traditionally called indicatives and non-indicatives. I believe that a well-developed theory of performatives will exhibit those differences in their proper perspective; I also think that the notion of "literal implementation" of a rule of information, together with the notions of non-deceiving and reliable performance of communicative acts, might be of some value in spelling out the idea that some sentences are "verifiable by their use", and in this way play a part in the definition of the class of performatives.

CHAPTER V

INTENTION-DEPENDENT EVIDENCE

V.1. BENNETT'S DEFENCE OF THE GRICEAN THEORY

The core of the Gricean theory is the alleged distinction between natural and non-natural meaning; the argument of Chapter I aimed, in part, to raise doubts about the basis of that distinction. In Bennett (1976), however, it receives an improved and considerably modified interpretation. In this section, therefore, I make some comparisons between Bennett's position and my own; page references will now be to Bennett's book, unless otherwise specified; exposition of Bennett's views will be confined to a bare minimum.

In which ways might *b* try to get *a* to believe that *p*? *b* might present *a* with something which itself gives evidence that *p* is the case; for example, *b* might show *a* a piece of film in which *c* is clearly to be seen in intimate relation with *a*'s wife, thereby getting *a* to believe that his wife has been deceiving him. But *b*'s arranging in *this* sort of way for *a* to have evidence of the truth of *p* would obviously not involve *b*'s meaning that *p*, or so Bennett maintains (p. 12). In this case *b* would be providing *a* with evidence which *naturally* means that *p* — something which is itself a sign of, or symptom of, the truth of *p*. According to Bennett, Grice "... uses 'non-natural meaning' for the sort which is involved when a person, rather than an event or fact or state of affairs, means that *p*" (p. 12). So non-natural meaning seems to pertain to some special kind of way in which a person tries to get someone to believe something. Bennett uses the following kind of example to introduce this special way: suppose that *b* and *a* are watching an opera, *a* looks across to *b*, their eyes meet, and *b* then grimaces exaggeratedly and holds his nose; given that *a* now believes that *b* meant that he was hating the performance, the question to ask is how *b* managed to produce that effect in *a*. The answer is that *b* intended to get *a* to think that he (*b*) hated the performance and intended to produce this effect by getting *a* to realize that this *was* his (*b*'s) intention. At least, *b* intended that *a*'s awareness of *b*'s intention to produce in him the belief that he (*b*) hated the opera was meant to be part of *a*'s reason for coming to believe that *b* did hate the opera. What we have here is an outline and unrefined presentation of what it is for *b* to try to get *a* to believe that *p by relying on the Gricean mechanism*; Bennett also notes

110

that the evidence presented by b to a was what he describes as *intention-dependent* evidence, in as much as the fact that b's grimaces and nose-holding counted as evidence depended essentially on the intentions b had in performing them. As I understand it, we are here asked to suppose that if b had not intended, by grimacing and holding his nose, to produce in a the belief that he hated the opera performance, then his (b's) grimacing etc. would not have constituted evidence that he hated the performance.

It is important to note (and Bennett does point this out) that a's belief that b is intending to produce in him the belief that b hates the performance is likely to be effective in producing the latter belief in a only if a also believes that b is not trying to deceive him and that b is well informed. In my terms, a must trust that b's gestures and grimacing are non-deceiving and that they are reliable. For the case at hand it is, of course, reasonable to assume that b *is* reliably informed — surely *he* knows whether or not he hates the performance — but that is just an incidental feature of this particular case.

Bennett also notes that ". . . in the opera example nothing like conventional meaning is involved. Gestures like . . . [this] . . . are in common use; but their success as vehicles of meaning does not depend on that, for someone might understand such a gesture perfectly on his first encounter with this sort of behaviour" (p. 14). Nevertheless, he *is* prepared to admit that communications of this sort "succeed only because they contain an iconic element"; b's act provided "a natural pointer to the meaning"; it was performed "in a manner significantly *like* an unaffected display of a certain kind of aesthetic displeasure" (*loc. cit.*).

This last point, taken seriously, provides the key to an alternative account of this example; it seems to me that we may represent what is meant by the claim that an iconic element is involved by interpreting the example as one in which b is making use of what he supposes to be an element of a's sign system, in my sense of that term, in order to *create a case of signalling*.

Recall that what was said in the earlier discussion of signs was that a might have good grounds for dropping a belief of type (I.1) if he thinks that b is aware that he (a) has that belief:

(I.1) $B_a((E_b p \cdot Z) \rightarrow q)$.

Since the sign is an action of b we may suppose it to be within b's power to make use of a's belief (I.1), once he is aware of it, to try to manipulate a's beliefs — perhaps in a way that would not meet a's interest in being informed.

It is not unreasonable to suppose that grimaces of certain sorts are a natural response, although perhaps not always or even often involuntary, to an unpleasant experience. In the case at hand, it may be assumed that *a* and *b* mutually believe that, in certain circumstances, grimacing may be taken as a sign of experiencing something unpleasant. But given that we allow that *a* is not a totally gullible member of the opera-going public, then it is most likely that he does not believe that whenever *b* grimaces in a certain way whilst watching the opera that actually is a sign that he (*b*) feels that the performance is dreadful. Nevertheless, it would still be reasonable for *b* to assume — in virtue of their shared belief about a connection between grimacing and an unpleasant experience — that *a* would take any *non-deceiving* performance by him of the act of grimacing, in this situation, as a sign that *b* felt that the opera was awful.

On what kinds of grounds would *a* be justified in accepting *b*'s act as non-deceivingly performed? In the light of the earlier discussion (above, section III.5), it is clear that *a* must be satisfied that *b* *intends to implement* that element of their shared sign system according to which it is often the case that one who grimaces is experiencing something he considers to be unpleasant; it will not be *relevant* for *a* to consider whether *b*'s act was non-deceivingly performed unless he attributes an intention of this sort to *b*. But — as was also noted in the earlier discussion — *a*'s belief that *b* has this intention will by no means be *sufficient* to justify his accepting *b*'s performance to be non-deceiving. Unless he *is* totally gullible, *a* will see that the issue of the trustworthiness of *b*'s communicative act remains an open one; however, the point to be emphasized is that the further aspects of the situation, which *a* *does* need to consider in making up his mind about *b*'s trustworthiness, need have *nothing* to do with whether or not *b* has intentions of the specifically Gricean kind: considerations of *that* sort need not be relevant.

My suggestion is, therefore, that what happens in the opera example is that *a* believes that *b* non-deceivingly exploits a belief they share about what grimacing is often a sign of; *a* need attribute to *b* no *other* intention than that *b* intends that his act of grimacing be seen as an instance falling under the generalization connecting grimacing and having an unpleasant experience. *That* intention is *not* the same as an intention of the specifically Gricean kind; the Gricean mechanism has been undercut — for, quite independently of it, an explanation can be given of how *b*'s act enables *a* to arrive at the conclusion that *b* thinks that the opera-performance is dreadful.

As I understand Bennett, he would accept this last conclusion, but he would nevertheless want to insist that a weaker Gricean mechanism, which he calls "sub-Gricean", is at work in the opera example; *and* he takes the sub-Gricean factor to be present in all cases where *no* iconic element is involved and in all cases in which, as I would put it, there is no exploitation of a *sign* system. The sub-Gricean factor is operative in all types of communication.

His position may be explained in the following way: first, he imagines "a powerful, semantically structured communication-system" called *Plain Talk* (p. 169) which he takes to be distinct from human languages only in ways which are "small and trivial" (p. 170); plain-talkers do not have intentions of the specifically Gricean type: "... when they utter intending to communicate, they do not rely for success on the operation of the Gricean mechanism in their hearers" (*loc. cit.*). They rely instead on beliefs held by the audience to the effect that whenever such-and-such an act is performed then such-and-such a state-of-affairs obtains.

Now Bennett's sub-Gricean conditions are supposed by him to provide the proper diagnosis of the differences between the cases of *natural* and *non-natural* meaning presented in Grice's 1957 paper. In each of the cases Grice rejects as instances of non-natural meaning, the communicator is offering *intention-free* evidence that a particular state of affairs obtains, whereas, for the accepted cases, he takes himself to be offering intention-dependent evidence for some state of affairs. There is no need, Bennett maintains, to assume that the communicator has the full range of Gricean intentions — that he is relying on the Gricean mechanism — the weaker condition will suffice (p. 171).

I next quote Bennett at some length to show how these elements of his theory link up:

"Gricean and sub-Gricean conditions part company when applied to a case where U utters S intending to communicate P, this being an implementation of Plain Talk . . . In such a case . . . the Gricean conditions are not satisfied, because A has a route from 'S is uttered' to 'P is true' which by-passes the lemma 'U intends to communicate P'. Yet the sub-Gricean conditions are satisfied, because the only evidential link between S and P is an intention-dependent one. When A moves from 'S is uttered' to 'P is true' on the strength of some generalization approximating to 'Whenever S is uttered P is true', he follows a route which does not include any thought about U's intention; but the route nevertheless depends on U's intention, because if U had not intended to communicate P when he uttered S, it would have been inappropriate to bring his uttering S under the generalization that whenever S is uttered P is true. The crucial background fact is that the generalization is true only because of the intentions of past S-utterers: the general link between S-uttered and P-true owes its existence to one link between S-uttered and intention-to-communicate-P, and a second link between intention-to-communicate-P and P-true. So if someone uttered S without intending to communicate P, it would be a sheer coincidence if on that occasion P were true. Therefore, if U utters S without intending to communicate P, and A infers from this that P is true because in his experience whenever S is uttered P is true, the inference is not unreasonable but it is nevertheless vitiated by error. And that gives the content to my claim that A's route from 'S is uttered' to 'P is true' is, whether or not he realizes it, an intention-dependent one, or that the uttering of S is intention-dependent evidence that P is true" (p. 172).

According to earlier remarks (pp. 127–28) Bennett means by "intention to communicate P", "intention to get someone to believe that P".

Of course Bennett is right to insist that before an act of b can justifiably be taken by a to be evidence that q, on the strength of some generalization a believes to obtain (connecting performance by b of the act and the truth of q), it must be appropriate for b's act to be brought under the generalization; and it will be appropriate for this to be done only if b had certain intentions in performing the act. Essentially the same point emerged from my account of the opera example, and the same point again applies where the generalizations concerned are what I have chosen to call "rules of information".

In Section III.5 I tried to specify more closely what intentions it is that b has when it *is* appropriate to classify an act of his as an instance of implementation of a rule of information. On Bennett's account it would seem that b must intend to get his audience to believe that q; according to my position, Bennett's account here says both too much and too little: it says too little because it totally ignores non-literal implementation of the covering rule or generalization; it says too much because b may intend literal implementation of the rule without caring in the least whether a actually accepts the truth of q — he *need* intend no more than that a should form the belief that, according to his (b's) information, q is true; a will form that belief if he accepts that b's performance is non-deceiving — hence the earlier suggestion, in section III.5, that b's act is intended as a literal implementation of a rule of information only if he intends to produce in a the belief that his (b's) act of communication is non-deceivingly performed.

Since the present concern is Bennett's "Plain Talkers", mention of non-literal implementation of the covering generalizations is beside the point. Confining attention, then, to the literal instances, the conclusion to be drawn at this stage is that I agree with Bennett that the communicator must be supposed to intend his act to be taken as instantiating the relevant generalization — if the act is to be taken as providng evidence that q. I disagree with Bennett merely with respect to the precise way in which that intention of the communicator is to be characterized. So the question now is: is this *all* that is involved in the claim that the evidence provided by the communicator is *intention-dependent* evidence? If it is, then the Gricean theory has been reduced to a mere shadow of its former self — to the really rather unexciting observation that, for example, my putting my right arm out of the right-hand side window of my car whilst driving along the highway counts as evidence that I am about to turn right only if I intended, in performing the arm-movement, to implement the rules of traffic signalling.

However, the above-quoted passage from Bennett reveals, I think, that there is more to his sub-Gricean conditions than this. For it appears that Bennett is raising *two* issues in that passage, the *first* of which is that the utterance must be supposed to be an instance of implementation of the "S is uttered — P is true" generalization before it can be thought to provide evidence that P, and the *second* of which concerns something more substantial: "The crucial background fact is that the generalization is true only because of the intentions of past S-utterers . . .". Although I find Bennett's meaning difficult to discern, in the remainder of that passage, it seems to me that he is there raising the issue of what the *grounds* are upon which speakers and hearers may justify their acceptance of the truth of the "S is uttered — P is true" generalizations. I take it that he is concerned with *grounds* rather than with the *actual origin* of such generalizations — despite his reference to "past S-utterers" — because he says elsewhere that he does not believe that consideration of the actual origins of communication systems will necessarily lend support to the Gricean theory; (see p. 206, where he says that it is not the case that ". . . something Gricean must be involved at least in the beginnings of any intentional communication-system").

If this interpretation of Bennett is correct — and there are also other passages which strongly suggest that it is (e.g., p. 175, second paragraph) — then it appears that the most substantial issue with which he is concerned pertains to the grounds upon which meaning generalizations are established. In exploring this issue he first moves in the direction of Lewis's theory of convention (see Bennett's Chapter 7). But, as he soon points out, if it is assumed that all meaning generalizations are grounded on Lewis conventions then he is back with the problem of the Plain Talkers, because (as I mentioned in Chapter I) Lewis has proved, at least for conventional signalling systems, that behaviour in conformity to convention is behaviour which relies on the Gricean mechanism. (It is worth pointing out that Bennett does not regard the communicative behaviour of Plain Talkers as in any sense eccentric or unusual: ". . . Plain Talk captures a high proportion of what actually goes on at the linguistic centre" (p. 182).)

I shall follow the details of Bennett's argument no further; my main point has been to locate the two types of issue to which the notion of intention-dependent evidence, which forms the basis of his revised account of Grice, is relevant. The first type of issue pertains to the intentions of a communicator in implementing a meaning generalization, and its counterpart in my theory is the account of implementation of rules of information. The second issue pertains to the grounds upon which meaning generalizations are established, and its counterpart in my theory would concern the grounds upon which the members of some population base those beliefs which characterize the rules of information of the language and signalling systems they use. As I have already said (above, p. 25), I do not want to commit myself to any specific analysis of this second issue — but perhaps some further speculations relating to it are in order.

Posed in terms of a and b's mutual belief of type (I.25) (p. 24, above), the key question will now be this: on what grounds do a and b take b's non-deceiving performance of $E_b p$ in Z as a sign that $V_b q$? Do they think that it just happens to be the case that a non-deceiving performance of that sort is a sign that $V_b q$, just as a, in the earliest example, may have believed that it just happened to be the case that when b took a walk it was 3 o'clock? That suggestion seems quite ridiculous, as would the proposal that they believe the connection between $E_b p$ (in Z) and $V_b q$ to be like the connection between clouds and rain, or like that between colouration on the bark and disease in the tree. *This* is where the kinds of consideration raised by Grice and Bennett *are* relevant; and this is where one can see the full point in talking about *intention-dependent* evidence. What then is the "nature of the connection" between $E_b p$ (in Z) and $V_b q$? Not "it happens to be that . . ." and not "it is causally necessary that . . ." — so what kind of modality is involved? The answer is I think, the modality Shall; for beliefs in connections of this type are *grounded upon* beliefs about the intentions and normative expectations of agents.

How precisely to articulate, in terms of Shall and the other modalities, the structure of the beliefs I suppose agents to have as grounds for beliefs of type (I.25), I am not certain. Perhaps these grounds may be described as mutual beliefs about what the audience is (normatively) expected to believe when he is confronted by a non-deceiving performance of such-and-such an act, performed in such-and-such circumstances; in which case they may be represented formally by (V.1):

(V.1) $B_{ab}^{*}(((E_b p \cdot Z) \cdot O_a(E_b p \cdot Z)) \rightarrow \text{Shall } E_a B_a V_b q)$.

In conformity with what has gone before, I continue to use Shall to operate on act-descriptions; a wff of type $E_a B_a p$ may be understood as describing a's act of *deciding that p* is the case. According to the terminology used in Pörn, 1977, sections 12 and 13, a wff of type (V.2) expresses a *norm-*

(V.2) $p \rightarrow \text{Shall } E_a q$;

accepting that terminology, (V.1) may be said to express a mutual belief in a norm: it entails, by the logic of mutual belief, a (normative) expectation which b has of a and an intention of $a;$ b expects a to decide that (according to the information available to b) q is true, on the condition of b's non-deceiving performance of $E_b p$ (in Z); and, on the same condition, a intends to decide that, according to the information available to b, q is true.

The phrase "intends to decide" may sound strange, but there is really nothing unusual involved in the idea it expresses; as a matter of fact, agents do operate plans for processing the information they receive, including plans pertaining to what is to be taken as counting as evidence for what.

The kinds of grounds a and b have for maintaining mutual beliefs of type (V.1) may be assumed to pertain to the fact that behaviour in conformity to the norm contained in (V.1) will be behaviour which meets their interest in transmitting and receiving information; the norm describes a way in which they can coordinate their behaviour so that this interest of theirs may be satisfied.

I end these speculations here. The case against the Griceans with respect to what meaning *is* remains, but I accept the relevance of a notion of intention-dependent evidence to the description of the grounds upon which agents base the beliefs expressed in rules of information. I make no claim to the effect that (V.1) captures precisely what *Bennett* means by "intention-dependent" evidence; in fact I suspect that (V.3) might come closer than (V.1) to incorporating within my approach the intuitions Bennett has about intention-dependent evidence:

(V.3) $B_{ab}^{*}(((E_b p \cdot Z) \cdot O_a(E_b p \cdot Z)) \rightarrow \text{Shall } E_b B_a V_b q)$.

My reason for preferring (V.1) to (V.3) is that in one sense (V.3) presupposes (V.1); for if b succeeds in conforming to the norm embodied in (V.3), and thus brings it about that a believes that $V_b q$, then, in normal circumstances, he will have been able to achieve that result because *a has decided*, on the basis of b's communicative act, that $V_b q$; that is, b succeeds in conforming to the norm embodied in (V.3) *because a* conforms to the norm embodied in (V.1).

Summing up, it may be said that I have distinguished three questions:

(i)   what are meanings?

(ii)   what kinds of beliefs must agents be supposed to have in virtue of which it is possible for them to communicate with one another?

(iii)   what grounds can the agents be supposed to have for the beliefs mentioned in (ii)?

My answer to (i) follows Lewis; rules of information form the core of my answer to (ii); and a tentative answer to question (iii) has been offered in the form of (V.1).

V.2. THE MODALITY SHALL AND THE ANALYSIS OF SIGNALLING

One question which arises quite naturally out of the discussion in the last section is this: could the role played in my theory by rules of information have been played equally well by some other expression, in which my deontic operator does not appear, but in which the modality Shall is employed? It is clear that I think that the answer to that question is negative; but it is also clear that the lack of a fully developed account of the grounds of rules of information leaves my theory exposed to the *possibility* that a description of those grounds could be given independently of the concept expressed by my deontic operator — in which case, presumably, communication situations could be described in terms of the grounds agents have for accepting rules of information, rather than in terms of the rules of information themselves, thus again avoiding the need for the deontic operator.

My own view is that the notions of non-deceiving performance of communicative acts and of trust of type no-deceit are quite indispensable, and that their analyses cannot be formulated in terms of the modality Shall; one reason for believing this is that Shall is used in the description of agents' intentions, and among the acts which agents perform intentionally are acts of communication which are themselves designed to deceive; that perhaps rather obscure point should become clearer in due course.

There are some suggestions about how Shall can be used in the analysis of signalling (and with no recourse to a deontic operator) in Pörn, 1977, Section 36; but those suggestions are of limited interest for the present discussion, because Pörn is there concerned with the rather special type of situation in which an agent is (normatively) expected to signal whichever one of a range of situations he is in. It is clear that that kind of situation is not typical of communication in general; b may be very tired today, but it is not expected of him, necessarily, that he should communicate that fact to anyone.

Of considerably greater interest, however, are the proposals for the analysis of signalling made in Pörn, 1979, Section I. He there specifies the paradigm of a signalling norm as having the following form:

(V.4) $(t) (\sim p_t \rightarrow \text{Shall} \sim q_t)$

where p_t says that the state of affairs described by p obtains at time t, and q_t says that the signalling action described by q is performed at that time. Given that May is the dual of Shall, (V.4) is equivalent to (V.5):

(V.5) $(t) (\text{May } q_t \rightarrow p_t)$.

The act described by q is said to be a sign which non-naturally means that p according to a signalling system, if and only if a norm of form (V.4), linking p and q, belongs to that system.

The difficulty, inherent in this approach, to which I want to draw attention may be brought out by asking how it can cope with the kind of situation in which a signaller intends to mislead or deceive by means of his performance of a signalling act. Let it be supposed that b believes that his hoisting a flag $(E_b q)$ is a sign which, according to some signalling system, means that the enemy is coming (p). Pörn's proposals might now be thought to require that (V.6) is true:

(V.6) $B_b(t) (\sim p_t \rightarrow \text{Shall} \sim E_b q_t)$.

Let it also be supposed that b believes that, at some particular time t_1, the enemy is not coming; i.e.,

(V.7) $B_b \sim p_{t_1}$.

And, finally, suppose that b intends to hoist the flag (at t_1) if the enemy is not coming at t_1; according to Pörn's own analysis of intention, this last supposition should be represented by (V.8):

(V.8) $B_b(\sim p_{t_1} \rightarrow \text{Shall } E_b q_{t_1})$.

But (V.8) is not consistent with the conjunction of (V.6) and (V.7), assuming − with Pörn − that (Q.Ser) holds for R(Shall). So it seems that this approach does not permit this commonplace situation to be consistently described.

However, the account of norms and intentions given in the second chapter of Pörn (1977) provides good reasons for thinking that Pörn would object to the idea that (V.6) properly represents b's belief that the norm expressed by (V.4) is a member of a signalling system. He in fact goes to some lengths to distinguish between beliefs which characterize intentions and beliefs that a norm is valid or in force.

He first characterizes the notions of *normative system* and *validity in a set of norms*; suppose that a class K of norms is given, then the following procedure may be used to define the class S_K of norms, where S_K constitutes a *normative system with base K*:

1. K is a subset of S_K.
2.   If p represents the formulation of some norm or set of norms in S_K, and q represents a norm formulation which is entailed by p (in virtue of some presupposed set of logical truths), then the norm expressed by q is also a member of S_K.
3.   Nothing else is a member of S_K.

A norm N is now said to be *valid in* a set K of norms if and only if it is a member of the normative system which is based on K, i.e., a norm N is valid in K iff $N \in S_K$. (This definition is obviously designed to include the kind of case in which a norm, although not explicitly stated in a set of norms, may nevertheless be said to be valid in that set, in virtue of being derivable from it.)

Thus b's belief that the norm expressed by (V.4) is valid or in force in a signalling system will not be represented by (V.6); it is properly thought of, according to Pörn, as a belief that the norm expressed by (V.4) is a member of the set of norms which constitute the signalling system. The way is now left open for a consistent formalization of the situation in which b intends to deceive in his performance of a signalling act.

The above characterization of a normative system takes an initial set K of norms as given — as the basis of the system. But just what is involved in the claim that a base set of signalling norms is taken as "given" or "existing"? For Pörn the answer seems to be that the members of the base set exist if and only if they are the product of an act of decision, and have not subsequently been rejected in a decision of type cancellation. His earlier (1970) "realist" conception of norms, which focussed on punitive reaction, is now replaced by an alternative "realist" conception of norms, which focusses on another type of action — namely, *decision* to admit or reject a norm.

The difficulty which I find in this, from the point of view of the present discussion, is that Pörn represents an agent's act of deciding to do q if p by means of (V.9):

(V.9) $E_a B_a(p \to \text{Shall } E_a q)$

and (V.9) entails (V.10), which says that a intends to do q if p:

(V.10) $B_a(p \to \text{Shall } E_a q)$.

From this it will of course follow that the problem about describing the situation in which b intends to deceive (in his performance of a signalling act) will re-appear, *if* b's belief that the signalling norm expressed by (V.4) belongs to a set of existing signalling norms is itself grounded upon an act of decision (to admit the norm) *performed by b himself*. So the conclusion would appear to be that if b exploits the norms of a signalling system for the purpose of deceiving then, on Pörn's account, the existence of the exploited norms *cannot* be the product of b's agency. This seems to me to be a curiously inflexible situation; surely an agent may be party to the setting up of a signalling system which he then proceeds to exploit for the purpose of deceiving (among other purposes, perhaps)?

The kind of dilemma which Pörn's approach seems to be liable to fall into can be avoided, of course, if the rules constituting a signalling system are thought of not as norms (pertaining to what shall or shall not be done in particular circumstances) which the users of the system believe to be in force, but as mutually held beliefs about what is true in those circumstances in which the performance of the signalling acts is optimal, or ideal, in a certain specifiable sense. (My rules of information have *notional* existence, i.e., they exist as the objects of mutually held beliefs of the members of the population who use the signalling system.) The independence of that concept of optimality from the modality Shall permits a highly flexible analysis of the decisions, intentions and normative expectations of agents who exploit the rules of the signalling system for various purposes.

I do not wish to give the impression that I view this issue as settled; on the contrary, I have only shown (if my argument is correct) that this particular way of analysing signalling in terms (essentially) of the normative modality, and in the absence of a deontic modality, is problematic. To the extent that other patterns of analysis are possible, the issue is still very much an open one.

In conclusion I mention one other type of issue which remains to be confronted by Pörn's approach: what is it which distinguishes those sets of norms which constitute signalling systems from other sets of norms? It may be said that signalling systems are those sets of norms the elements of which can be used in the task of *indicating*, but if that were to be the criterion (and Pörn does not in fact propose it as the criterion), then an account of indicating would be required which did not presuppose that the acts performed by the signaller were meaning-bearing signs; for the point of the criterion would be to distinguish between norms which *do* confer meaning on the actions to which they pertain and norms which *do not*.

Perhaps the criterion can easily be stated for those acts which involve delivering the sentences of some language; any norm regulating an act of that sort will be a signalling norm (a suggestion of that sort is I think implicit in Section II.3 of Pörn, 1979). But what, then, of non-verbal signalling acts? Suppose that there is a norm of type (V.5) in force, to the effect that students may take the exam only if they have registered for the course; how, on Pörn's account, are we to know that this is not a component element of a signalling system, and that therefore a student's taking the exam is not to be interpreted as a sign which non-naturally means that he has registered for the course?

The counterpart to this issue in my theory lies in the fact that I needed a specific notion of optimality to characterize the rules of information of a signalling system — not just any sense of "ought" would do; and in Chapter II an attempt was made to specify the nature of that modality more fully in terms of its relation to the modalities B_a and V_a. My suspicion is that Pörn's approach will require a distinction between two types of Shall; but then there would be little, if anything, gained, by way of descriptive economy, in adopting Pörn's approach rather than mine.

CHAPTER VI

THE DOUBLE BIND

VI.1. GENERAL FEATURES OF A DOUBLE-BIND SITUATION

In 1956 a research group led by Gregory Bateson published a paper entitled "Toward a Theory of Schizophrenia"; this paper soon came to exert considerable influence on thinking about schizophrenia, and on the general approach to the understanding of mental illness. Perhaps the most striking aspect, at that time, of the Bateson group's approach was that they tried to make sense of the strange communicational behaviour they observed in schizophrenics in terms of an hypothesis about the type of interpersonal context in which the schizophrenic acquired his/her communicative abilities. The conjecture was that the communication pattern of the schizophrenic, although seeming to be peculiar in "ordinary" contexts, must nevertheless have been learned in a setting within which it could be seen as fitting. The schizophrenic, it was claimed, ". . . must live in a universe where the sequences of events are such that his unconventional communicational habits will be in some sense appropriate" (Bateson *et al.*, 1956, p. 177).

The main purpose of the 1956 paper was to attempt to characterize certain essential features of these "sequences of events" — to identify key aspects of the communicational and interactional pattern in relation to which the schizophrenic's own style of communication had been developed. To name this set of features, they coined the term "double bind"; the elements of the double bind were described as follows:

(a) Two or more persons are involved; in the earliest formulations, one of these is said to be the "victim" on whom the double bind is inflicted by the binder or binders. Typically, but not always, the setting is the family, the victim is one of the children, and the mother inflicts, or plays a part in inflicting, the double bind. (Later formulations, e.g., Weakland, 1960, p. 25, suggest that the victim soon learns to send reciprocal double-bind messages of his/her own, so that it is in fact more appropriate to describe all those involved in the maintenance of the double-bind pattern of communication as victims of that pattern. See also Bateson *et al.*, 1963, p. 58. I shall not dwell on this point, since it is of only marginal interest in relation to the criticism to be developed later in this chapter.)

(b) One of the persons involved – the one designated "victim" in the first formulations – is the recipient of two conflicting injunctions; these injunctions conflict in that they logically cannot both be obeyed. Furthermore, in both the earlier and the later formulations, it is stressed that these two injunctions are on different levels; the one injunction is a meta-injunction in relation to the other; alternative descriptions employed are that the one injunction is on a "more abstract" level than the other, and that the two injunctions are of different "logical types". It is this part of the characterization of the double bind which will be the focus of the critical discussion later in this chapter; it needs clarifying, and is intimately connected with the underlying approach to communication theory adopted by the Bateson group, who maintained that their theory was based upon Russell's Theory of Logical Types (Bateson *et al.*, 1956, p. 174).

(c) The person receiving the conflicting injunctions ". . . is involved in an intense relationship" (Bateson *et al.*, 1956, p. 180) with the person or persons issuing the injunctions; he/she is thus anxious to determine correctly the nature of the messages sent, and to respond appropriately and in a way which will not undermine or damage the relationship.

(d) (Closely connected with point (c)) – the recipient of the conflicting injunctions is prohibited from "leaving the field". That is, he/she is not allowed to step outside the dilemma, rejecting the problem posed by the conflicting injunctions. Inasmuch as "leaving the field" constitutes making a comment *about* the conflicting messages, fulfilment of this condition is guaranteed by the requirement that the recipient make no metacommunicative statement (Bateson *et al.*, 1956, p. 180; Watzlawick *et al.*, 1968, pp. 212–213).

(e) The kind of situation described in (a)–(d) is a recurrent feature of the interaction pattern of the parties concerned. This point relates particularly to the hypothesis regarding the pathogenicity of the double bind: "Our hypothesis does not involve a single traumatic experience, but such repeated experience that the double bind structure comes to be an habitual expectation" (Bateson *et al.*, 1956, p. 178).

In order to exemplify the kind of interaction pattern involved, the Bateson group supplied the following illustration from clinical data: "A young man who had fairly well recovered from an acute schizophrenic episode was visited in the hospital by his mother. He was glad to see her and impulsively put his arm around her shoulders, whereupon she stiffened. He withdrew his arm and she asked, "Don't you love me any more?". He then blushed, and she said, "Dear, you must not be so easily embarrassed and afraid of your feelings"." (Bateson *et al.*, 1956, p. 188). The writers add that the young man was able to stay with his mother only a few minutes longer, and that after her departure he assaulted a ward orderly.

A clearer understanding of this example becomes possible if it is viewed against the background of the hypothesis the Bateson group proposed concerning the family situation of the schizophrenic. The most striking characteristic of this situation is that the "... mother becomes anxious and withdraws if the child responds to her as a loving mother" and that she also finds these feelings of anxiety and hostility to be themselves unacceptable (Bateson *et al.*, 1956, p. 184). Her strategy for denying these feelings is to simulate a loving attitude towards the child in order to persuade him/her to relate to her as to a loving mother. She makes it clear that the child's failure to respond appropriately to this persuasion would meet with her disapproval; but, of course, if the child does comply that will again arouse her anxiety and hostility. It is further supposed that there is nobody in the family able to intervene in support of the child in its attempts to come to terms with the mother's contradictory attitudes.

As far as the Bateson group was concerned, the key point about a situation of this kind is the following: the mother will transmit to the child messages of at least two types — messages of a hostile or withdrawing nature in response to the child's approaches, and messages which simulate a loving attitude, intended to deny her hostility and transmitted in response to the child's response to that hostility. The group stressed that they took these messages to be of different orders, or, as they also put it, of different logical types. "The important point is that her loving behaviour is ... a comment on (since it is compensatory for) her hostile behaviour and consequently it is of a different *order* of message than the hostile behaviour — it is a message about a sequence of messages. Yet by its nature it denies the existence of those messages which it is about, i.e., the hostile withdrawal" (Bateson *et al.*, 1956, p. 185).

By one means or another the child will be prevented from commenting on the contradictory nature of the mother's position; in particular, the mother may make it clear to the child that metacommunication of this sort would represent a threat to their relationship, because it would suggest that he/she doubted her sincerity. Indeed the conjecture is that the repeated experience of the double-bind communication pattern prevents the child from learning to metacommunicate properly; it fails to learn the normal procedures for finding out what others really mean by what they say, whether they can be taken seriously, and so on. In addition, the child's own capacity to express what *he/she* really means is impaired.

Thus, in summary, the central hypothesis as regards the communicational behaviour of schizophrenics takes the following form: given that a child learns its basic communicational skills in interaction situations characterized by the persistent occurrence of double binding, then the result is likely to be that he/she fails to discriminate accurately what people mean by what they say and do; "... he would not share with normal people those signals which accompany messages to indicate what a person means. His meta-communicative system – the communications about communication – would have broken down, and he would not know what kind of message a message was" (Bateson *et al.*, 1956, p. 182). And such behaviour, the group believed, is typical of schizophrenics; the authors also expressed this by saying that, typically, schizophrenics have difficulty in distinguishing between *orders* of messages, that they have "... special difficulty in handling signals of that class whose members assign Logical Types to other signals" (Bateson *et al.*, 1956, p. 177).

My account has still not spelt out in full the group's views concerning the connections between the Theory of Logical Types and the phenomenon of the double bind; to that problematic issue I return in Sections VI.3 and VI.4. I want first to show how the conceptual framework and formal language developed in earlier chapters may be applied to the analysis of the "illustration from clinical data".

VI.2. THE ILLUSTRATION FROM CLINICAL DATA –
A FORMAL DESCRIPTION

From the logical point of view, the interesting question about the mother-son example concerns the nature of the impossible or untenable situation which the son finds himself in. What sort of inconsistency or incongruity confronts him? How is it to be characterized?

There are no doubt various ways in which the interaction sequence might be interpreted; I shall here attempt to stay close to the line of interpretation which the Bateson group appear to have adopted.

The first important step in the interaction is that the boy signals affection to his mother by hugging her. In terms of the framework developed earlier in this book (see especially Section I.3) the son's act may be seen as an instance of implementation of a rule of information (VI.1), in which $E_b p$ describes the son's act of putting his arm around his mother's shoulders, b is the son, a the mother, Z describes relevant contextual factors, and q describes the state of affairs that the son wishes to show his mother affection:

(VI.1) $B^*_{ab}(((E_b p \cdot Z) \cdot O_a(E_b p \cdot Z)) \to V_b q)$.

Since the interpretation given to the interaction assumes that the mother's subsequent act of "stiffening" is a response to the son's display of affection, it must be taken for granted that the mother *trusts* the boy's signalling act to be both non-deceiving and reliable (for these distinctions, see Section III.1) and thus that $B_a q$ is true. (It is worth noting in passing here that the formal language is rich enough to permit description of a strange but conceivable variant of this situation: the case in which the mother has managed to convince herself that she is better informed than her son is about what he wants and does not want; she might then accept that his act of hugging her was non-deceivingly performed – in which case $B_a V_b q$ would be true – without also believing that q. Accounts given in the literature on the mothers of schizophrenics suggest that this conjecture is by no means farfetched.)

The next stage in the interaction – the mother's stiffening – is interpreted as a signal from the mother (or perhaps as a sign) that the son is to stop hugging. Where $E_a r$ describes the mother's act of stiffening, and this is viewed as a case of signalling, then the act may be seen as an instance of implementation of (VI.2):

(VI.2) $B^*_{ab}(((E_a r \cdot Z') \cdot O_b(E_a r \cdot Z') \to V_a E_a$ Shall $E_b \sim E_b p)$.

(Among the things here described by the context indicator Z' will be the fact that b is in the process of performing the act described by $E_b p$. On the analysis of imperative signalling, see Section IV.1, above.) According to my account of *sincerity* for imperative signalling acts, a is sincere in her performance of the act $E_a r$ given that she expects (in the normative sense) that b shall obey the imperative; i.e., in this case, sincerity requires that a has the following belief: B_a Shall $E_b \sim E_b p$. The interpretation the Bateson group gives to this phase of the interaction sequence surely requires that the son believes that the mother has this expectation – indeed, that will be his reason for stopping the embrace. Thus $B_b B_a$ Shall $E_b \sim E_b p$ is true.

If it is supposed that the mother's "stiffening" response to the son's display of affection is a response which it is really beyond her power to control, then, in terms of the discussion in Chapter I, her act should be viewed as a (mutually recognized) sign, and (VI.2) should be replaced by (VI.3):

(VI.3) $B^*_{ab}((E_a r \cdot Z') \to s)$.

Here the supposition is that s describes the circumstance that a feels uncomfortable, anxious, displeased, etc. The son forms the belief that s on the basis of (VI.3) as soon as $B_b(E_a r \cdot Z')$ is true; the notions of deceit and reliability do not enter the picture. It may then be assumed that, on the grounds of his belief that s, the son forms the belief that his mother expects him to stop hugging her; that is, the outcome is again that $B_b B_a$ Shall $E_b \sim E_b p$ is true.

The next step is that the boy performs the act described by $E_b \sim E_b p$ — that is, he stops hugging his mother — in fulfilment of what he takes her expectation to be.

The structure of the dilemma facing the son begins to unfold at the next stage, when the mother says to him, questioningly, "Don't you love me any more?". The Bateson group suggest that part of what is involved here is that the mother is telling the boy that she believes that he does not wish to express affection to her. That is, according to this interpretation, the mother is acting *as if* the boy's act of withdrawing his arm is an instance of implementation of the following rule of information:

(VI.4) $B_{ab}^* (((E_b \sim E_b p \cdot Z'') \cdot O_a(E_b \sim E_b p \cdot Z'')) \rightarrow V_b \sim q)$.

Furthermore, she is making it clear to the boy that she took his act of withdrawing his arm to be a non-deceiving and reliable performance (in relation to (VI.4)), on the basis of which she formed the following belief: $B_a \sim q$; she does not, in fact, have this belief, for, as was seen from the analysis of the first phase of the interaction, $B_a q$ is true. But her strategy is to *impose* on his act of withdrawing his arm an interpretation which will lead the *son* to believe that she believes that he does not wish to show her affection; thus, as I understand the group's view of this part of the interaction, the crucial outcome is that the boy forms the following belief: $B_b B_a \sim q$.

Now, according to elementary properties of the logic of belief, b cannot *both* believe that a believes that $\sim q$ *and* believe that a believes that q. Therefore, if the son has (quite correctly) drawn the conclusion from the first phase of their interaction that his mother took his act of hugging her to be a non-deceiving and reliable implementation of (VI.1), then he will now have to revise that view; the mother is effectively forcing him into adopting a distorted, incorrect view of what occurred in the first phase. And what alternative interpretations are open to him? Given that he does not step outside the dilemma by making the judgement that his mother is misleading him, he might deny that hugging is a way of expressing affection (*cf.* Bateson *et al.*, 1956, p. 189) — but this of course will conflict with what he has learnt about the ways in which affection is expressed in his culture; or he might perhaps retain the belief that hugging is a means of showing affection, but deny that *he himself* is capable of expressing affection by that means: here he would be doubting his own ability to convey his meaning to others through normal channels; or, again, he might begin to doubt whether he really had wanted to express affection to his mother: perhaps, he might think, mother knows better than I do what I want and feel — perhaps she accepted that my act of hugging was non-deceiving, and so formed the belief that, *according to the information available to me*, I wished to show her affection (i.e., $B_a V_b q$), but nevertheless knew that I am not reliably informed about what I want, and so she did not believe that I really did want to show her affection. The point, for the Bateson group, is of course that these ways of "resolving" the dilemma can be seen to correspond to characteristic features of schizophrenic behaviour. Prevented from maintaining a correct perception of the situation, the way out for the son is that he ". . . sacrifices himself to maintain the sacred illusion that what the parent says makes sense. To be close to that parent, he must sacrifice his right to indicate that he sees any metacommunicative incongruencies, even when his perception of these incongruencies is correct" (Bateson, 1960, p. 208).

The misery of the son's situation is compounded by the last significant phase of the interaction sequence. His mother's closing remark, to the effect that he should not be afraid of expressing his feelings, serves as an imperative, enjoining him to express affection towards her. But the supposition is, of course, that *any* other attempt on his part to show her affection — by hugging her, or by any other means — will re-start the cycle, for it will lead to her "stiffening" response and, subsequently, to her trying to cover up her inability to accept displays of affection from him. Any attempt on the son's part to ignore the mother's "stiffening" response is likely to be unsuccessful: the conjecture is that she is the kind of woman who cannot tolerate such displays; it will be made clear to him that his attempts to show affection incur her displeasure; equally, she communicates to him that his ceasing to display affection also incurs her displeasure. "The impossible dilemma thus becomes: "If I am to keep my tie to mother, I must not show her that I love her, but if I do not show her that I love her, then I will lose her."" (Bateson *et al.*, 1956, p. 190).

As was pointed out earlier, the Bateson group's account of the key features of the double bind emphasizes that there will be two injunctions, *on different levels*, which conflict with one another; in the present case, the injunction on the lower level will be that expressed through the mother's stiffening response

to the son's display of affection; the higher-level injunction will be that
expressed by the mother at the end of the sequence, when she tells the boy
not to be afraid of expressing his feelings. Perhaps the idea is that this second
injunction can be thought of as an injunction on a *higher* level than the first
because it pertains to a *class* of acts — namely, the class of acts of displaying
affection — whereas the first injunction pertains only to *one member* of this
class. Thus, the higher-level injunction encourages the performance of any
member of the class of acts of showing affection, whereas the lower-level
injunction forbids the performance of one member of that class. There is
no doubt that the two injunctions conflict with one another, and no doubt
that, seen as just described, they are on different levels. But I would dispute
the claim that the conflict itself *arises from* any *confusion* of levels. The
conflict arises from the fact that the higher-level injunction, if accepted by
the boy as sincere, will convey to him that his mother expects him to perform
any members he might care to choose from the class of acts of expressing
affection, whereas the lower-level injunction, if accepted by the boy as
sincere, conveys to him that his mother expects him to refrain from hugging
her; so, *if* the boy accepted that his act of hugging *was* a genuine and successful expression of affection, his mother's injunctions would appear to him
to conflict — she would seem to him to have expectations of an irrational,
unreasonable kind; (as has been shown, the mother's basic strategy is to
try to prevent the boy from reaching and/or maintaining this (correct)
diagnosis of the situation.) The mother's normative expectations are irrational in the sense that they violate the requirement of consistency imposed
by adopting seriality for the relation R(Shall) — see above, pp. 52, 99,
101.

The reason for emphasizing that the conflict between the higher and
lower-level injunctions does not arise from the difference in levels itself
is that it is precisely here that the most unsatisfactory part of the Bateson
group's analysis emerges; for they appear to maintain that the difference in
levels is a crucial factor: they suggest that the source of the conflict resides
in a *paradox* of the kind which Russell's Theory of Logical Types, and its
extension to a theory of levels of communication, is designed to resolve;
they believe that the root of the double bind lies in the confusion of different
logical levels.

The examination of this claim leads directly to Bateson's views concerning
the structure of communication, which are the focal point of the next section. Meanwhile, it is worth noting that the analysis given in this section
of the illustration from clinical data shows that the conflict between the two

injunctions is only *part* of the story; other factors must also be included in the full characterization of the nature of the son's predicament. And this will remain true regardless of how the structure of the conflict between the two injunctions is analysed.

VI.3. BATESON'S THEORY OF COMMUNICATION

According to Haley's account of the development of the double bind project, it was partly for practical reasons that, in 1954, the group made *schizophrenic* communication the focus of their attention (Haley, 1976, pp. 64–65). Their earlier research had been wider in scope, and concerned paradoxes in communication in general, with special reference to the Theory of Logical Types; but their grant for that research was not renewed – instead, they got financial support for a project on schizophrenic communication. In a later note on the double bind, written in response to the treatment the theory had been receiving in the literature, the Bateson group stressed the fact that a proper assessment of the double-bind approach to the understanding of schizophrenia could only be made within the terms of the general theory of communication from which the work on schizophrenia had been developed (Bateson *et al.*, 1963, p. 56). They pointed out that a whole range of communicational phenomena had been investigated in relation to this more general, underlying theory, including metaphor, humour and play; the patterns of communication in the families of schizophrenics provided just one area of application of the theory; and the theory itself was said to be based upon the Theory of Logical Types. In his 1963 review of research on the double bind, Watzlawick made a similar point: "Very few of the references to the double bind theory deal with what its originators consider the essential concept, i.e., the *Theory of Logical Types*" (Watzlawick, 1963, p. 65). Others writing in this area have made essentially the same complaint – and there can be little doubt that it is justified.

In the context of the present essay, it is Bateson's underlying theory of communication, rather than its relevance to the understanding of schizophrenia, which is of primary interest. This is so largely because, in my opinion, his theory exhibits confusions and obscurities which tend to hide the key insight which Bateson had into the nature of signalling acts. I shall try to argue that much of what Bateson was essentially concerned with may be reformulated in terms of the distinctions made earlier in this book. But the important point is *not* whether my interpretation of Bateson's intentions is correct; regardless of that issue, I can still present a case for maintaining that a good deal of the communicational behaviour which has been discussed in the literature under the heading of "double bind" may be quite systematically accommodated within the framework I have proposed — and it may be described, in part at least, with the aid of the modal-logical tools developed in Chapter II.

The conceptual framework from which the theory of the double bind was developed is summarized in "A Theory of Play and Fantasy" (Bateson, 1955; see also the outline account in Haley, 1976, pp. 60–64).

To repeat: Bateson *insisted* that his approach to the understanding of communication was derived from Russell's Theory of Logical Types, and its extension to a theory of levels of language (due to Ramsey, Tarski and Carnap — *cf*. Reichenbach, 1947, p. 225). He emphasized that human communication always operates ". . . at many contrasting levels of abstraction" (Bateson, 1955, p. 150); he was particularly concerned to draw attention to metacommunicative levels by means of which communicators may show whether their acts of communication are to be taken seriously, jokingly, sarcastically, as gestures of friendliness, as acts of aggression, . . . and so on. Indeed, he suggests that an important stage in the evolution of communication occurs when the organism comes to recognize and to employ metacommunication of this sort, i.e., ". . . when the organism gradually ceases to respond quite "automatically" to the mood-signs of another and becomes able to recognize the sign as a signal: that is, to recognize that the other individual's and its own signals are only signals, which can be trusted, distrusted, falsified, denied, amplified, corrected and so forth" (Bateson, 1955, p. 151).

It appears that a key development in his thinking about these matters resulted from his observation of animal behaviour, in particular of *play* of a certain kind, in which the actions performed were similar to, but not the same as, those employed in fighting. "Now, this phenomenon, play, could only occur if the participant organisms were capable of some degree of metacommunication, i.e., of exchanging signals which would carry the message "this is play"" (Bateson, 1955, p. 152).

It seems here that Bateson is concerned to draw attention to the characterization problem which provided the dominant theme of Sections I.2 and I.3, above — namely, the task of characterizing the essential differences between signs and signals; to this point I shall return again below.

But problems and confusion enter, I feel, in the next phase of Bateson's argument, when he turns to the analysis of the message "This is play". His reasoning here seems to me to be somewhat obscure, and for fear of misrepresenting it I quote it in full. Concerning the message "This is play", he says that it "... contains those elements which necessarily generate a paradox of the Russellian or Epimenides type — a negative statement containing an implicit negative metastatement. Expanded, the statement "This is play" looks something like this: "These actions in which we now engage do not denote what those actions *for which they stand* would denote.""

"We now ask about the italicized words, "*for which they stand*". We say the word "cat" stands for any member of a certain class. That is, the phrase "stands for" is a near synonym of "denotes". If we now substitute "which they denote" for the words "for which they stand" in the expanded definition of play, the result is: "These actions, in which we now engage, do not denote what would be denoted by those actions which these actions denote." The playful nip denotes the bite, but it does not denote what would be denoted by the bite.

"According to the Theory of Logical Types such a message is of course inadmissible, because the word "denote" is being used in two degrees of abstraction, and these two uses are treated as synonymous. But all that we learn from such a criticism is that it would be bad natural history to expect the mental processes and communicative habits of mammals to conform to the logician's ideal. Indeed, if human thought and communication always conformed to the ideal, Russell would not — in fact could not — have formulated the ideal" (Bateson, 1955, pp. 152—153).

One criticism which might immediately be offered here concerns Bateson's choice of the phrase "for which they stand" in his first expansion of the statement "This is play". Why suppose that playful nips "stand for" genuine bites — why not simply say that they resemble them?

But even if this criticism is ignored and one proceeds to the second expanded version of "This is play", it remains doubtful whether the statement, thus formulated, violates the constraints which the Theory of Logical Types would impose. Surely, the second expansion might be construed in the following way: on the highest level — (1) — are the acts of playful nipping which are said to denote acts of serious/genuine biting, which are on level (2); the latter, in turn, denote aggression, hostility, and so on, the "items" of the lowest level, (3). Items on level (1) do not denote items on level (3). Violation of the kinds of constraints which a theory of types or levels would impose *would* arise *if*, e.g., an item on level (1) were *also* assumed to be a member of the class of items on level (2). *Then* paradox would result, because one and the same act would both denote and not denote an item on level (3). But I see no reason why the original statement *must* be interpreted in such a way as to involve this kind of confusion of levels and the consequent generation of paradox; nothing forces one to assume that an item on level (1) must also be a member of the class of items on level (2).

Furthermore, I am puzzled as to why Bateson found it necessary to formulate these expansions of the statement "This is play". After all, the *potential* for paradoxical interpretation of this statement lies clearly on its surface, just as it does in the case of the statement "This statement is false". Paradox arises if the message "This is play" is itself included in the class of items to which the term "this" is assumed to refer. Of course there is no denying that an interpretation of this kind, involving as it does a confusion of levels, *might* be made; if the class of actions referred to by the signal "This is play" included that signal itself, then it would no longer be clear that that class of actions could be assumed to be play; for the point of metacommunicating the signal "This is play" in relation to a class of actions would be undermined if that metacommunication were not taken seriously, i.e., if it were not taken as not-play.

Perhaps it is even the case that animals in the wild confuse levels of message in the kind of way which gives rise to paradox. It is however hard to imagine that such confusion could be widespread or persistent (among animals in the wild), for it is difficult to conceive of any survival value which might attach to the persistence of such patterns of interpretation. This point should be clearly contrasted with the fact that it is very easy to imagine the potential value to a species of a system of communication complex enough to permit signalling, involving, as it would, a metacommunicative level on which such factors as trust and deceit play a decisive role.

In a letter to Norbert Wiener in 1954, part of which is reproduced in Haley (1976, p. 66), Bateson says of the message "this is play" that it ". . . can be exchanged non-verbally between mammals and . . . when it occurs it is usually implicit in those meaningful actions which are qualified by the statement "this is play". The message "this is play" thus seems to qualify itself and something like an Epimenides paradox arises". By saying that the message is "implicit" in the meaningful actions which it qualifies, does Bateson mean that it is not distinguishable, as an aspect or part of those meaningful actions? It may often be difficult for the *human observer* of animal behaviour to perceive clearly the difference between message and meta-message, but it seems reasonable to assume that the animals themselves will have developed rather clear ways for indicating to one another when a message is to be taken as playful — especially when the play-behaviour itself resembles combat and a severe penalty attaches to mis-reading the metacommunicative cues.

What seems so peculiar about Bateson's position is that he appears to maintain that metacommunicative messages of the type "This is play" *must* generate paradoxes of the Russellian or Epimenides type. In the passages already quoted, and again at the end of the 1955 essay, he ties the violation of logical type or level theory with the very *possibility* of signalling: "Our central thesis may be summed up as a statement of the necessity of the paradoxes of abstraction. It is not merely bad natural history to suggest that people might or should obey the Theory of Logical Types in their communications; their failure to do this is not due to mere carelessness or ignorance. Rather, we believe that the paradoxes of abstraction must make their appearance in all communication more complex than that of mood-signals, and that without these paradoxes the evolution of communication would be at an end. Life would then be an endless interchange of stylized messages, a game with rigid rules, unrelieved by change or humour" (Bateson, 1955, p. 166; *cf.* Bateson, 1956, p. 197). (Note that Bateson here uses the term "mood-signal", whereas he earlier (page 151 of the same essay) employed the term "mood-sign"; it is clear, however, that in both cases he is talking about *signs* in the sense of Chapter I.)

My main point, in relation to Bateson, is first to agree that signalling involves communication on at least two levels: it follows from my account of the characterization of signalling acts that an audience, receiving a signal, will be concerned to determine *both* the meaning of the signal *and* whether the signaller's performance of the signalling act can be taken as non-deceiving; both of these factors are likely to play a part in the audience's assessment of what the signaller *meant by* performing the signalling act (*cf.* Chapter III, especially sections 1 and 4). Equally, the signaller will be conveying two levels of message – the one concerning the content of the communication, the other a metacommunication about the signalling act, concerning whether the act constitutes a literal or non-literal implementation of the governing rule of information (*cf.* Section III.5, above).

It now also follows – from the fact that these two levels exist in any signalling act, the one level being a metacommunication in relation to the other – that the *possibility* is created for what Bateson calls the paradoxes of abstraction to arise; if part of a signalling act conveys the message "this signal is not to be taken literally", then of course the same sort of paradox *could* arise as was seen to be *possible* in the case of the message "this is play". But where Bateson is quite wrong, it seems to me, is in his contention that paradoxical results of this sort *must* arise. Furthermore, although I do not wish to deny that such paradoxes may play a role in certain forms of humour, in certain types of schizophrenic communication, and perhaps in other uses of communication too, I *do* want to suggest that much metaphoric, ironic, sarcastic, humourous and playful usage of communication is achieved by exploiting the dual/multi-level nature of communicative acts in ways which *cannot* be analyzed in terms of the paradoxes arising from *confusion* of levels. For instance, much humorous use of language derives from the fact that it is possible to "say one thing and mean another", and I tried to show, in Section III.4, *how* this is possible. But the explanation did not need to call on the notion of paradox.

In addition, I believe that essentially the same point can be made, against Bateson, with respect to many of the examples of the double bind cited in the literature. (See below for further discussion of this.)

In summary, Bateson overestimated the importance of the Russellian and Epimenides type of paradox to the analysis of communication; and he underestimated our capacity to exploit the existence of levels of communication in ways which have nothing to do with such paradoxes. It would not, I think, be unfair to suggest that Bateson's preoccupation with these paradoxes side-tracked him from the original task — which was to give an adequate characterization of the difference between signs and signals.

Some of his remarks concerning this task seem to fit in with my own position rather well. Consider the passage already quoted from page 151 of his 1955 essay, and the following: "It seems to me that when the human species ate of the fruit of the Tree of Knowledge, it discovered that automatic signs could be turned into signals and emitted with conscious or unconscious purpose. With that discovery, of course, also came the possibility of deceit, and all sorts of other possibilities" (Bateson, 1956, pp. 157–158). Bateson did not, however, go one step further and use the notion of the possibility of deceit as a defining characteristic of signals (as contrasted to signs).

Bateson's distinction between the "report" and "command" aspects of a communicative act provides a further point of contact between his approach and mine (Watzlawick *et al.*, 1968, pp. 51–52). It seems to bear some likeness to my distinction between, on the one hand, the meaning of a signal, and, on the other hand, those factors which are involved in determining what a signaller means by employing a signal having that meaning. Thus the "report/command" distinction seems to be a step in the direction of a fuller characterization of signalling. (See also Bateson, 1967, pp. 102–106.)

A more comprehensive account of Bateson's framework would have to include discussion of his distinction between analogic and digital communication, and of his hypothesis that there is a hierarchy of levels of *learning*. I shall not develop these points here, but will simply assert that I do not believe that these other aspects of his approach provide grounds for undermining my main line of argument in this section.

I have attempted here to point to similarities between Bateson's claim that any communicative act is performed on various levels, and my own characterization of signalling actions. One question which naturally arises in this connection is the following: if part of what is involved in signalling is that the signaller sends a metacommunication concerning whether or not his act of signalling may be taken literally, must there not then also be rules of information governing the performance of the metacommunicative signalling acts? Consider, for example, the types of facial expression which convey the message that an act of communication is to be taken literally; surely, given the way rules of information have been characterized, facial expressions succeed in performing this function only if they themselves are taken as non-deceivingly performed. Will there not then be signals which accompany, or are aspects of, the expressions of the face, and which serve to indicate whether these expressions can be trusted — and must not these signals also be governed by their own rules of information . . . and so on?

Each signalling act, of course, is governed by the rule of information which its performance implements; however, the above line of argument, leading to the hierarchy of rules of information, also assumes that it will always be another *signal* which is employed to indicate whether or not a given signal can be trusted; and that assumption is not always correct, for there are at least two other sources of information which an audience may make use of: first, they may consider information they may have about the communicator (whether he has been shown to be trustworthy in the past, and so on), information they may have about matters relating to the subject of his communication (whether what he is trying to tell them is compatible with reliable information they may already have), and information they may have about the context in which the act of communication occurs (whether, in the particular circumstances, he is likely to be trying to mislead them). Secondly, the audience may derive information from *signs*; in this connection it is worth noting, with Bateson, that it takes a skilled actor to control the full range of those non-verbal metacommunicative indicators of trustworthiness. For very many people, much non-verbal metacommunication of this sort operates as a sign system, by and large beyond their power to control. And one who is skilled in such arts creates for himself a difficult situation, of course, if his skills come to be discovered for what they are; for he is then known to be able to manipulate those very devices which ordinarily serve as quite reliable indicators of a signal's trustworthiness; he will be forced to try to find other ways of getting people to take his acts of communication seriously. (*Cf.* Bateson, 1968, p. 388. There is much more to be said on these matters, in relation to both the social psychology and the evolution of communication systems. Bateson's 1968 essay raises a number of interesting issues in these areas.)

VI.4. THE DOUBLE BIND AND LEVELS OF COMMUNICATION

Returning now to the analysis of the double bind, and in particular to the illustration from clinical data discussed in Section VI.2, the question may be raised again as to whether the notion of different *levels* of communication is relevant to understanding the nature of the son's predicament. The passage from page 185 of the Bateson group's original paper, quoted above on page 125, is just misleading, hinting as it does that a paradox of the Epimenides kind lies at the heart of the matter; but if, as I have suggested, one ignores Bateson's preoccupation with such paradoxes, and focusses instead on the characterization of signalling, does the clear role *there* played by the notion of levels of communication help to improve the analysis of this example of the double bind?

I believe that it does; it has been pointed out that contextual features are among the features which will be taken into account in making judgements about the trustworthiness and sincerity of (verbal or non-verbal) signalling acts. Within the mother-son example, the context for the evaluation of any one of the signals consists, in part, of the *other* signals which also belong to the sequence, (or, rather, to the "cycle"). Viewing the situation from the boy's side, it is clear that if he decides in relation to *any* of his mother's signals that *it* is trustworthy/sincere, then his evaluation of some *other* aspect of the cycle immediately runs into difficulties. For example, if he trusts his mother when she indicates that she believes that he does not want to show her affection, then, as was shown in Section VI.2, the boy has to conclude that his attempted communication of affection by hugging was — for some reason or other — unsuccessful. Conversely, if he believes that his act of hugging her was indeed a way of communicating to her his affection, and that she also accepted that it was, then he is forced to the conclusion that, if he has understood her question "Don't you love me any more?", she must be trying to deceive him. Furthermore, it seems that he can take her "stiffening" response to his embrace as indicating that she expects him to refrain from embracing her if and only if he does not accept that she is sincere when she enjoins him to show her affection; unless, of course, he again concludes that his act of hugging her did not count as a genuine expression of affection – but then let him try any other signal of affection, and the trouble will recur.

The upshot of this account is that there is a clear sense in which it may be said that each signal in the cycle *disqualifies* another signal. No coherent set of metacommunicational judgements, pertaining to the trustworthiness/ sincerity of the messages, is available to the son, unless he either concludes that his mother is irrational or untrustworthy (which would constitute a threat to their relationship), or else distorts his own perception of the situation. The problem lies on the metacommunicational level – the level of judgements about whether the signalling acts can be trusted or taken to be sincere. In this respect there is some degree of similarity between this way of analysing the mother-son double bind and the account given in Section III.2 of Moore's puzzle about saying and disbelieving.

The following example may also serve to bring the present discussion more into line with what was said in Chapter III: ". . . suppose that a mother said to her child, "Come and sit on my lap." Suppose also that she made this request in a tone of voice which indicated she wished the child would keep away from her. The child would be faced with the message, "Come near me," qualified incongruently by the message, "Get away from me." " (Haley, 1959, p. 168; the example is taken from a passage in which Haley is speculating about the kind of pattern of family interaction which might be supposed to encourage typically schizophrenic communicational behaviour.) It is obvious that tone of voice functions as a metasignal, indicating how a spoken message is to be taken; so this is a case in which one aspect of a verbal signalling act (the tone of voice) disqualifies another aspect (the literal meaning of the sentence spoken). In this respect the example resembles some of those considered in Chapter III, where I imagined situations in which it is made clear to an audience that a particular act of communication cannot be taken literally, (i.e., it cannot be taken to be a non-deceiving implementation of the rule of information concerned – *cf.* Section III.5) and in which the communicator intends the audience's awareness of the non-literal nature of his performance to play a part in their interpretation of that performance. He is trying to indicate to the audience that what he means by performing the act is not to be identified with the meaning of the signal transmitted: they must find some other explanation of what *he* means, although their knowledge of the meaning of the signal transmitted may help them to reach that explanation. He is perhaps joking, playing, teasing, being ironic, sarcastic

... and so on. He is exploiting the incongruence of the two levels of his act of communication in order to try to get his own meaning across.

Now, returning to Haley's example, it would seem that a perfectly normal audience reaction to that act of communication would be to take it as a non-literal performance and to try to work out what the communicator meant by it; but *that* is just where the normal situation and the double bind situation would differ − for the assumption is, in Haley's example, that there is not *anything else* which the mother *means by* performing the speech act, she is not encouraging the child to look for some *other* meaning; indeed, as is characteristic of the double bind situation, the child would be punished for attempting to step "beyond" or "outside" the framework of the communication situation itself; the child is not allowed to ask, e.g., "What do you mean? Are you teasing me, or what?" It is as if the mother is performing an act of communication which can only be taken non-literally, but, at the same time, is forcing the child to accept it as if it *could* be taken literally. And that, I suspect, is the crux of the double bind.

Essentially the same point may be made in relation to the mother-schizophrenic son example, despite the fact that the pattern of communication there exhibits a more complex constellation of incongruence and disqualification. If the son takes any of his mother's communications at its face value, then, so long as he assumes that his mother is sincere, and reasonable in her demands, he will be able to make coherent sense of the situation only if he distorts his perception of it. The sane, but forbidden, response would be to step outside the framework imposed by his mother and by his relationship to her, and to confront her with the following choice: either to explain what she really means by her eccentric pattern of communication, or else to accept that her hypocrisy has been recognized for what it is.

One of the merits of this way of analysing the double bind, it seems, is that it brings out its similarities to, and differences from, certain types of non-literal usage of communication involved in some forms of play, humour, metaphor, etc. This lends support to Bateson's claim that a theory of communication which took proper account of *levels* of communication ought to be able to throw light on the whole range of such phenomena.

Those familiar with the literature in this field might wish to point out that this way of interpreting the core of the double bind corresponds quite closely with the view adopted by those who have focussed on Bateson's distinction between "report" and "command" aspects of communication, rather than on his preoccupation with paradox. (See, e.g., Olson, 1972, especially pp. 80−84.) The present account, however, derives from a critical appraisal of Bateson's underlying communication theory, and provides a new framework for the characterization of signalling, in terms of which the role of different levels may be articulated more explicitly.

For those who are less familiar with the literature, it is perhaps worth stressing that the view has *persisted* among double bind theorists — it seems to have become the received view — that the core of the phenomenon lies in paradox, of which paradox of the Russellian or Epimenides kinds is usually taken to be the model. (See, e.g., Watzlawick *et al.*, 1968, Chapter 6; Abeles, 1976, pp. 117—119; Haley, 1976, especially pp. 71—72.) One striking feature of the statements of the received view which I have read is that not one of them (since the original 1956 paper) has produced a detailed analysis of the mother-schizophrenic son illustration from clinical data; and so none of them manages to show that the paradoxes are in the least relevant to that example.

Patterns of communication involving paradox of the Russellian or Epimenides kinds, and perhaps of other kinds, may well be of interest in the analyses of humour, the behaviour of schizophrenics and psychotherapeutic techniques. What is regrettable, of course, is that the term "double bind" has been applied here too, thus obscuring important differences from the cases considered above.

The idea that the literature contains at least two distinct definitions of the double bind has also been proposed in Guindon (1971). (I rely here on the reports given in Abeles, 1976, pp. 135—136, and in Sluzki and Ransom 1976a, pp. 156—157.) Guindon considered, on the one hand, the kind of case in which the content of a verbal message is incongruent with the tone of voice in which it is uttered, and, on the other hand, messages involving logical paradoxes, defined in terms of internal inconsistency within the verbal channel alone. Although I would of course favour a distinction along these lines, the earlier discussion makes it clear that the former category provides only a partial characterization of (that type of) double bind; for there is an important difference between the kind of situation in which discrepant levels of communication put an audience in an untenable position, and the kind of situation in which a communicator exploits level discrepancy in, e.g., joking and playing. Acceptance of this point would seem to diminish the value of Guindon's empirical work, which attempted to investigate the hypothesis that the two types of double bind, as defined by Guindon, are differentially pathogenic.

The results of the discussion in this chapter suggest that those engaged in communication-oriented psychopathological research might find it instructive to look more closely at the precise roles of trust, reliability and sincerity in the pragmatics of human communication — perhaps particularly in cases where it might otherwise have been taken for granted that paradoxes deriving from problems of self-reference provide the key to an adequate analysis. Despite the fact that it tends strongly towards the received view of the nature of the double bind, the account of paradoxical communication given in Watzlawick *et al.* (1968, Chapter 6), offers one final illustration of this point. Having first discussed double binds ("paradoxical injunctions", as they call them), the Watzlawick group go on to consider "paradoxical predictions", and there the focus of attention is on one version of the "unexpected examination" paradox. What is of interest in relation to their discussion of this paradox is that they *do* attempt to bring out the role played by assumptions about *trust*: "The dilemma would be . . . impossible if the students did not trust the headmaster implicitly. Their entire deduction stands and falls on the assumption that the headmaster can and must be trusted. Any doubt of his trustworthiness would not dissolve the paradox logically, but would certainly dissolve it pragmatically. . . . So we reach the conclusion that not only logical thinking but also trust make one vulnerable to this kind of paradox" (Watzlawick *et al.*, 1968, pp. 223–224). But why did the group not pursue the same line of enquiry in relation to the double bind itself?

It is worth noting here that Binkley has produced an analysis (using techniques of modal logic) of what appears to be essentially the same version of the "unexpected examination" paradox as that discussed by Watzlawick *et al.* Interestingly, Binkley's conclusion is that his version of the paradox may be seen to belong to the same family as Moore's paradox (Binkley, 1968, p. 135); and in Section III.2 I showed how that paradox can be analyzed in terms of assumptions about trust and sincerity.

These comments are not intended to imply that all versions of the "unexpected examination" paradox can be properly analyzed independently of consideration of the role of self-reference. Indeed, Montague and Kaplan (1960) have shown that some — but not all — versions do turn on the issue of self-reference.

Obviously, what is going to be required is a more elaborate classification of types of communication situation, and of types of paradox, before a proper assessment can be made of the role of paradox in the pragmatics of human communication. A comparable view has been expressed by Dell (1981), whose main concern is with the use of paradox in psychotherapy, an idea in which there has been a great deal of interest in recent years, particularly in the wake of the double bind theory. Dell concludes that

". . . paradoxical therapy . . . remains a set of techniques in search of a theory" (p. 41). The title of his paper is intriguing: "Some *Irreverent* Thoughts on Paradox" (italics mine); this choice of adjective reminds one that ". . . an agnostic in the holy of holies doesn't get much camaraderie" (Albee, *A Delicate Balance*, Act I, p. 27), but it suggests too that maybe the time has come to step outside the framework — or is it, I wonder, a bind? — which the received view seems to have imposed.

CONCLUDING REMARKS

The literature on the philosophy of language is a jungle of some considerable density; the difficulty in negotiating a path through the area is due to (at least) the following two factors:

(i) Different types of questions about language and language use have often been confused with one another, with the result that there has been a fair amount of discussion at cross purposes; for instance, questions about what meaning is have often been confused with questions about how meanings are learnt. Too little attention has been paid to the general problem of characterizing the nature of language use.

(ii) Different contributions to the field are also hard to compare because of the lack of a uniform pattern of description of situations in which communication occurs, and because of the lack of a sufficiently precise language for formulating such descriptions.

This essay has attempted a classification of some key questions about language and language use, it has proposed a network of concepts for describing aspects of communication, and it has proposed a formal language rich enough to express that network. But it is obvious that the preceding chapters represent no more than a start − no more than preliminary groundwork. So, in conclusion, it is appropriate to make some suggestions about further lines of development.

(A) In Chapter IV it was mentioned, in passing, that the formal model will have to be strengthened if the *dynamics* of communication *processes* are to be adequately described. In Pörn (1977) there are, in addition to the modal-logical models, examples of the application of techniques from, e.g., games theory and cybernetics in the description of general aspects of the dynamics of social interaction; it is reasonable to assume that such models can also be usefully applied to the particular types of social interaction in which communication occurs.

A further reason for thinking that it might be instructive to look at communication processes from the point of view of the games-theorist is that the notion of *trust* plays such a prominent role in my framework; and, of course, it was the theory of games of coordination which provided Lewis's own point of departure (Lewis, 1969).

144

A very interesting account of the use of some techniques from cybernetics in the formal description of communication processes is to be found in MacKay (1972). Indeed, the general issue of the relationship between modal-logical description and the description of systems is a fascinating one (see, e.g., Pratt, 1980), and as regards the specific task of analyzing communication systems, the following hypothesis would seem worth investigating: that the modalities B_a, V_a, O_a and Shall may be understood as characterizations of components of the *governors* or *regulators* which help control the operations of systems engaged in enquiring and communicating — i.e., of systems engaged in seeking and transmitting information. The account of the modalities V_a and O_a, in Chapter II, suggested that the relevant possible worlds might themselves be interpreted as representing states of an enquiring system; there would appear to be scope for a potentially very fruitful combination of modal-logical and system-theoretic description in this area.

(B) The accounts presented above of communication situations — especially in Chapter III and VI — indicate clearly that a lot remains to be said about the means available to an audience for determining, or attempting to determine, what the communicator's intentions are; and more needs to be known regarding the various strategies available to the communicator for revealing and concealing his intentions. In other words, although I have said a good deal about the role of communicators' intentions, I have said little about the ways in which they are manifested and identified. This is of course a matter for empirical enquiry, but the hope is that the essay provides a conceptual framework in relation to which such an enquiry could be conducted systematically.

The issue under consideration here falls squarely within an area of social psychology known as "attribution theory", which has recently received a good deal of attention; work in this area is concerned with the processes whereby people attribute intentions, reasons and causes to the actions of others; (Shaver, 1975, gives an indication of some of the things going on in this field). Attribution theorists seem to be facing enormous conceptual problems, for they are taking on central issues in what philosophers usually call "the theory of practical reasoning", an area in which well-established results appear to be few and far between. My purpose, however, is again to point in the direction of applied modal logic, and thus to indicate a further respect in which the formal model might be extended. There is evidence already that modal-logical techniques can be usefully applied to problems in the theory of practical reasoning, e.g., Binkley (1965) and Pörn, 1977, Sections 16–18.

Some progress, surely, will have to be made in this field before any proper appraisal can be made of the Bateson group's conjectures about the learning history of the schizophrenic; for their point was, essentially, that the schizophrenic reveals in his/her communicational habits the consequences of being systematically deceived, misled and thwarted in his/her attempts to learn how to attribute intentions to communicators. So, as a prerequisite for evaluating their hypothesis, it will be necessary to identify the usual patterns which such attribution follows in the more "normal" learning history; classification and precise description is needed both of the strategies which communicators use to convey and disguise their intentions, and of the strategies which audiences use in their attempts to interpret these intentions.

These remarks should not be taken to imply that I think that all the interesting and important conceptual, descriptive and taxonomic problems can be settled from the armchair; I do not share the attitude of those philosophers who look with contempt upon the idea of "dirtying their hands with the empirical". The descriptive frame will almost certainly have to be modified in the light of empirical work; in genuinely *critical* science, the development of a sensitive conceptual apparatus will proceed in conjunction with empirical investigation. But, on the other hand, one must have *some* reasonably well-formulated descriptive/classificatory model before one can get going, just as one must have some hypotheses; and, as I have tried to indicate, this is likely to call for a more precise mode of description than that afforded by so-called "ordinary" language.

(C) It is clear that the proposals made in this essay are relevant to some central issues in the philosophy of the social sciences — issues which have figured prominently in the modern debate. I have in mind, in particular, the frequently made claim that a proper account of social action must incorporate an analysis of the meaning of that action to the participants, and the further claims, some of which seem to be rather obscure, about the ways in which an analysis of this sort relates to the explanation of social action. Unfortunately, much of the discussion in this area has been carried on in the absence of any clear specification of what it is to say that an action has a meaning or meanings; some of the ethnomethodologists would seem to be among the worst offenders here, and the cynic might be excused for thinking that this branch of sociology has been so named because it hath-no-methodology.

The suggestion has been made that concepts developed in speech act theory may be of use here (see, e.g., Skinner, 1972 and Habermas, 1970).

Habermas calls for a "theory of communicative competence", and some of what he says about competence of this kind suggests that the present essay constitutes a contribution to such a theory, inasmuch as I have attempted to characterize the beliefs agents have in virtue of which it becomes possible for them to communicate with each other. Furthermore, this essay has outlined key features of a class of meaningful acts — those used in communication — and it says in virtue of what it is that these acts can be said to have meaning; thus it should also provide the basis for determining what differences there may be between *understanding the meaning* of such acts and *explaining* them.

By this I do not want to suggest that the examples referred to in the literature in this area are always meaningful acts of the *communicational* type; on the contrary, it seems to me that one of the reasons why the discussion is often so vague is that there has been a tendency to assume that the class of meaningful acts can simply be identified with the class of intentional acts. But, surely, what is *again* needed here is a classification scheme, a taxonomy of meaningful acts; and the underlying descriptive problems are likely to be related rather closely to those of attribution theory, as well as to those of the study of signalling systems.

(D) Finally, mention should be made of some possible links between the dominant theme of Chapter I and the kind of approach taken to the analysis of meaning in game-theoretical semantics (see Saarinen, 1979). In Chapter I, I was concerned with the question of what it is for meaning-relations, between signs/signals and the world, to count as established. So the following remark by Hintikka, concerning the transition in Wittgenstein's philosophy of language, would seem to be closely relevant: "One especially instructive way of looking at Wittgenstein's development beyond the *Tractatus* is to emphasize the role of his insight into the need of analyzing those very representational relationships between language and reality which were left unattended to both in the *Tractatus* and in logical semantics. They are not natural relations. They cannot be gathered just by observing the expressions of the language and by observing the world they speak of. A visitor from Mars — or a child learning to speak — can only gather them from the behaviour of language-users. These representational relationships have as it were their mode of existence in certain rule-governed human activities. These activities are just what Wittgenstein calls *language-games*. They are what according to Wittgenstein creates and sustains the representative relationships between language and reality" (Hintikka, 1979a, p. 8). That is, the Wittgensteinian notion of language-game may provide the key to understanding what "creates and sustains" the relations between language and the world; furthermore, Hintikka believes that the semantical games of the games-theoretical semanticist are directly comparable to Wittgensteinian language-games (*op. cit.*, p. 19). Could it be then that the techniques of game-theoretical semantics would provide a valuable supplement to the formal methods used in Chapter I?

I do not know the answer to this question; but one reason for doubting whether an affirmative answer is correct is the following: as Hintikka points out (*op. cit.*, p. 11), the language-game idea is often employed by Wittgenstein in discussing how semantical relations are *learnt*; but if this is its primary use – i.e., if the language-game idea is really at home in the discussion of language *learning* – then it is not clear that it is relevant to my concerns. For my main interest has centred on a *different* question, pertaining to the characterization of what language-use *is*. This question is not only *different* from, but also *logically prior* to, questions about language learning, in the sense that we must know what it is to use a language before we can investigate how the use of language is learnt.

APPENDIX

(a) *Summary of readings for the main modal operators*:
In what follows, a and b designate any agents, and p and q describe any states of affairs:

$E_a p$:   "a brings it about that p".
$B_a p$:   "a believes that p".
$K_a p$:   "a knows that p".
$B^*_{ab} p$:   "a and b mutually believe that p".
$V_a p$:   "according to the information available to a, p is true".
$O_a p$:   "it is optimal (ideal) for a, relative to his interest in being informed, that p".
Shall p: "it shall be the case that p" (normative sense).

(b) *Some key formulae (numbered as in the text)*:

    (I.1) $B_a((E_b p \cdot Z) \rightarrow q)$.

Whenever (I.1) is true, then both of (I.2) and (I.3) are also true:

    (I.2) a takes b's bringing about p in circumstances Z as a sign that q;
    (I.3)   from a's point of view, b's bringing about p in circumstances Z means that q.

(I.15), below, is read "a intends to bring about p if q", and so it indicates how the modality Shall is used in the description of an agent's intentions:

    (I.15) $B_a(q \rightarrow \text{Shall } E_a p)$.

(I.25), below, represents the general form of what I call a *rule of information* for a and b, relative to b's bringing about p in circumstances Z. (Note that (I.25), (III.1) and (VI.1) are identical formulae):

    (I.25) $B^*_{ab}(((E_b p \cdot Z) \cdot O_a(E_b p \cdot Z)) \rightarrow V_b q)$.

(I.25) is read as follows: "a and b mutually believe that if b brings about p in circumstances Z and b's performance is non-deceiving (i.e., it is an optimal performance relative to a's interest in being informed), then, according to the information available to b, q is true".

The key notions of *trust* (both types) and *sincerity* are characterized —
in relation to the use/exploitation of rules of information — in Section III.1.

Finally, the basic logical form for an imperative is represented by (IV.1),
below, and is discussed in Section IV.1. It expresses the idea that b, who
issues an imperative to a, creates a normative relation between himself and a,
according to which a is to do p:

(IV.1) E_b Shall $E_a p$.

(c) *Some suggested introductory reading.*

A fine introduction to ordinary sentential logic and the logic of quantifiers
is Jeffrey (1981), especially for those who wish to proceed directly to modal
logic, since Jeffrey's semantical apparatus is a convenient point of departure
for semantical treatments of modalities.

Both Hughes and Cresswell (1968) and Chellas (1980) provide solid
introductions to modal logic, but the reader most interested in the kinds of
systems used in this book, or in Pörn (1977), might find the accounts of
semantical models given in the first three papers in Hilpinen (1981) to be
equally helpful.

Work is under way on an introduction to modal logic for social scientists,
with emphasis on the application of modal logic to the description of social
phenomena.

BIBLIOGRAPHY

Abeles, G.: 1976, 'Researching the Unresearchable: Experimentation on the Double Bind' in Sluzki and Ransom (1976), Chapter 7.

Albee, E.: 1966, *A Delicate Balance*, Penguin Books, Harmondsworth.

Andersson, J. S.: 1975, *How to Define 'Performative'*, Philosophical Studies, University of Uppsala.

Austin, J. L.: 1962, *How to do Things with Words*, Oxford University Press, Oxford.

Austin, J. L.: 1963, 'Performative-Constative', in C. E. Caton (ed.), *Philosophy and Ordinary Language*, University of Illinois Press, Urbana.

Bateson, G.: 1955, 'A Theory of Play and Fantasy', in Bateson (1973), pp. 150–166.

Bateson, G.: 1956, 'The Message "This is Play"', in Schaffner, B. (ed.), *Group Processes: Transactions of the Second Conference*, Josiah Macy, Jr. Foundation, New York, pp. 145–242.

Bateson, G.: 1960, 'The Group Dynamics of Schizophrenia', in Bateson (1973), pp. 199–214.

Bateson, G.: 1967, 'Style, Grace and Information in Primitive Art', in Bateson (1973), pp. 101–125.

Bateson, G.: 1968, 'Redundancy and Coding', in Bateson (1973), pp. 387–401.

Bateson, G.: 1973, *Steps to an Ecology of Mind*, Paladin, St. Albans.

Bateson, G. *et al.*: 1956, 'Towards a Theory of Schizophrenia', in Bateson (1973), pp. 173–198.

Bateson, G. *et al.*: 1963, 'A Note on the Double Bind – 1962', in Jackson (1968), pp. 55–62.

Bennett, J.: 1976, *Linguistic Behaviour*, Cambridge Univ. Press, Cambridge.

Binkley, R.: 1965, 'A Theory of Practical Reason', *Philosophical Review* **LXXIV**, 4, 423–448.

Binkley, R.: 1968, 'The Surprise Examination in Modal Logic', *Journal of Philosophy* **65**, 127–136.

Castañeda, H. N.: 1960, 'Imperative Reasonings', *Philosophy and Phenomenological Res.* **21**, 21–49.

Chellas, B. F.: 1980, *Modal Logic: An Introduction*, Cambridge Univ. Press, Cambridge.

Chisholm, R. M.: 1963, 'Contrary-to-Duty Imperatives and Deontic Logic', *Analysis* **24**, 33–36.

Clarke, D. S., Jr.: 1970, 'Mood Constancy in Mixed Inferences', *Analysis* **30**, 100–103.

Cooper, W. S.: 1978, *Foundations of Logico-Linguistics*, D. Reidel Publ. Co., Dordrecht, Holland.

Cresswell, M. J.: 1974, *Logics and Languages*, Methuen, London.

Danielsson, S.: 1973, *Some Conceptions of Performativity*, Philosophical Studies, Univ. of Uppsala.

Davidson, D. and Harman, G. (eds.): 1972, *Semantics of Natural Language*, D. Reidel Publ. Co., Dordrecht, Holland.

151

Dell, P. F.: 1981, 'Some Irreverent Thoughts on Paradox', *Family Process* **20**, 37–42.
Doreian, P.: 1970, *Mathematics and the Study of Social Relations*, Weidenfeld and Nicolson, London.
Espersen, J.: 1967, 'The Logic of Imperatives', *Danish Yearbook of Philosophy* **4**, 57–112.
Føllesdal, D.: 1967, 'Comments on Stenius's "Mood and Language Game"', *Synthese* **17**, 275–280.
Goffman, E.: 1970, *Strategic Interaction*, Basil Blackwell, Oxford.
Grice, H. P.: 1957, 'Meaning', *Philosophical Review* **66**, 377–88.
Guindon, J. E.: 1971, *Paradox, Schizophrenia and the Double Bind Hypothesis: An Exploratory Study*, Doctoral Dissertation, Univ. Washington, Univ. Microfilms, 71–28, 412.
Habermas, J.: 1970, 'Toward a Theory of Communicative Competence', in Dreitzel, H. P. (ed.), *Recent Sociology no. 2, Patterns of Communicative Behaviour*, Macmillan, New York, 1970.
Haley, J.: 1959, 'An Interactional Description of Schizophrenia', in Jackson (1968), pp. 151–170.
Haley, J.: 1976, 'Development of a Theory: A History of a Research Project', in Sluzki and Ransom (1976), Chapter 5.
Hansson, B.: 1974, 'A Program for Pragmatics', in Stenlund (1974), pp. 163–174.
Hilpinen, R. (ed.): 1981, *Deontic Logic: Introductory and Systematic Readings*, 2nd impression, D. Reidel Publ. Co., Dordrecht, Holland.
Hintikka, J.: 1962, *Knowledge and Belief: An Introduction to the Logic of the Two Notions*, Cornell Univ. Press, Ithaca, New York.
Hintikka, J.: 1979, 'Impossible Possible Worlds Vindicated', in Saarinen (1979), pp. 367–379.
Hofstadter, A. and McKinsey, J. C. C.: 1939, 'On the logic of Imperatives', *Philosophy of Science* **6**, 446–57.
Hughes, G. E. and Cresswell, M. J.: 1968, *An Introduction to Modal Logic*, Methuen, London.
Jackson, D. D. (ed.): 1968, *Communication, Family and Marriage: Human Communication Vol. 1*, Science & Behaviour Books Inc., Palo Alto, Calif.
Jeffrey, R. C.: 1981, *Formal Logic: Its Scope and Limits*, 2nd ed., McGraw-Hill, New York.
Jones, A. J. I.: 1970, *A Logic of Commanding*, unpublished M. A. thesis, Univ. of Birmingham.
Jones, A. J. I.: 1976, 'Generative Semantics: Some Test Cases', *Synthese* **32**, 293–307.
Jones, A. J. I.: 1980, 'Psychology and "Ordinary Language" – a Critique of Smedslund', *Scand. J. Psychol.* **21**, 225–229.
Jones, A. J. I.: 1981, 'On Describing Interpersonal Communication', in Pörn, I. (ed.), *Essays in Philosophical Analysis Dedicated to Erik Stenius on the Occasion of his 70th Birthday, Acta Phil. Fenn.*, Vol. 32, pp. 96–110.
Kanger, S.: 1972, 'Law and Logic', *Theoria* **38**, 105–132.
Lakoff, G.: 1972, 'Linguistics and Natural Logic', in Davidson and Harman (1972), pp. 545–665.
Lemmon, E. J.: 1962, 'On Sentences Verifiable by their Use', *Analysis* **22**.

Lemmon, E. J.: 1965, 'Deontic Logic and the Logic of Imperatives', *Logique et Analyse* **8**, 39–71.

Lewis, D. K.: 1969, *Convention: A Philosophical Study*, Harvard Univ. Press, Cambridge, Mass.

Lewis, D. K.: 1972, 'General Semantics', in Davidson and Harman (1972), pp. 169–218.

Lewis, D. K.: 1975, 'Language and Languages', in Gunderson, K. (ed.), *Language, Mind and Knowledge, Minnesota Studies in the Philosophy of Science*, Vol. VII.

MacKay, A. F.: 1969, 'Inferential Validity and Imperative Inference Rules', *Analysis* **29**, 145–156.

MacKay, D. M.: 1972, 'Formal Analysis of Communicative Processes', in Hinde, R. A. (ed.), *Non-Verbal Communication*, Cambridge Univ. Press, Cambridge, pp. 3–25.

Montague, R. and Kaplan, D.: 1960, 'A Paradox Regained', *Notre Dame J. of Formal Logic* **1**, 79–90.

Olson, D. H.: 1972, 'Empirically Unbinding the Double Bind: A Review of Research and Conceptual Reformulations', *Family Process* **11**, 69–94.

Pratt, V. R.: 1980, 'Application of Modal Logic to Programming', *Studia Logica* **XXXIX**, 2/3, 257–274.

Pörn, I.: 1970, *The Logic of Power*, Basil Blackwell, Oxford.

Pörn, I.: 1974, 'Some Basic Concepts of Action', in Stenlund (1974), pp. 93–101.

Pörn, I.: 1977, *Action Theory and Social Science: Some Formal Models*, D. Reidel Publ. Co., Dordrecht, Holland.

Pörn, I.: 1979, 'Meaning and Intension'; paper delivered to the Finnish-Soviet Logic Symposium, Moscow.

Reichenbach, H.: 1947, *Elements of Symbolic Logic*, The Free Press, New York.

Rescher, N.: 1966, *The Logic of Commands*, Methuen Monographs in Logic, London.

Ross, A.: 1944, 'Imperatives and Logic', *Philosophy of Science* **11**, 30–46.

Ross, J. R.: 1970, 'On Declarative Sentences', in Jacobs, R. and Rosenbaum, P. S., (eds.), *Readings in English Transformational Grammar*, Blaisdell, Boston.

Saarinen, E. (ed.): 1979, *Game-Theoretical Semantics*, D. Reidel Publ. Co., Dordrecht, Holland.

Searle, J. R.: 1969, *Speech Acts: An Essay in the Philosophy of Language*, Cambridge Univ. Press, Cambridge.

Searle, J. R. (ed.): 1971, *The Philosophy of Language*, Oxford Univ. Press, Oxford.

Sesonske, A.: 1965, 'Performatives', *Journal of Philosophy* **62**.

Shaver, K. G.: 1975, *An Introduction to Attribution Processes*, Winthrop Pub. Inc., Cambridge, Mass.

Skinner, Q.: 1972, ' "Social Meaning" and the Explanation of Social Action', in Laslett, P., Runciman, W. G., and Skinner, Q. (eds.), *Philosophy, Politics and Society*, 4th Series, Basil Blackwell, Oxford, pp. 136–157.

Sluzki, C. E. and Ransom, D. C. (eds.): 1976, *Double Bind: The Foundation of the Communicational Approach to the Family*, Grune & Stratton, New York.

Sluzki, C. E. and Ransom, D. C.: 1976a, 'Comments on Gina Abeles' Review', in Sluzki and Ransom (1976), Chapter 8.

Sosa, E.: 1966a, 'On Practical Inference and the Logic of Imperatives', *Theoria* **32**, 211–223.

Sosa, E.: 1966b, 'The Logic of Imperatives', *Theoria* **32**, 224–235.

Stenius, E.: 1967, 'Mood and Language-Game', *Synthese* 17, 254–274.

Stenlund, S. (ed.): 1974, *Logical Theory and Semantic Analysis*, D. Reidel Publ. Co., Dordrecht, Holland.

Strawson, P. F.: 1964, 'Intention and Convention in Speech Acts', *Philosophical Review*, Vol. 73.

Watzlawick, P.: 1963, 'A Review of the Double Bind Theory', in Jackson (1968), pp. 63–86.

Watzlawick, P. *et al.*: 1968, *Pragmatics of Human Communication: A Study of Interactional Patterns, Pathologies and Paradoxes*, Faber & Faber, London.

Weakland, J. H.: 1960, 'The "Double Bind" Hypothesis of Schizophrenia and Three-Party Interaction', in Sluzki and Ransom (1976), Chapter 2.

Åqvist, L.: 1965, *A New Approach to the Logical Theory of Interrogatives. Part I, Analysis*, Philosophical Studies, University of Uppsala.

Åqvist, L.: 1972, *Performatives and Verifiability by the Use of Language*, Philosophical Studies, University of Uppsala.

INDEX OF NAMES

155

INDEX OF NAMES

INDEX OF SUBJECTS

SYNTHESE LIBRARY

Studies in Epistemology, Logic, Methodology,
and Philosophy of Science

Managing Editor:
JAAKKO HINTIKKA (Florida State University)

Editors:
DONALD DAVIDSON (University of Chicago)
GABRIEL NUCHELMANS (University of Leyden)
WESLEY C. SALMON (University of Arizona)

1. J. M. Bochénski, *A Precis of Mathematical Logic.* 1959.
2. P. L. Guiraud, *Problèmes et méthodes de la statistique linguistique.* 1960.
3. Hans Freudenthal (ed.), *The Concept and the Role of the Model in Mathematics and Natural and Social Sciences.* 1961.
4. Evert W. Beth, *Formal Methods. An Introduction to Symbolic Logic and the Study of Effective Operations in Arithmetic and Logic.* 1962.
5. B. H. Kazemier and D. Vuysje (eds.), *Logic and Language. Studies Dedicated to Professor Rudolf Carnap on the Occasion of His Seventieth Birthday.* 1962.
6. Marx W. Wartofsky (ed.), *Proceedings of the Boston Colloquium for the Philosophy of Science 1961-1962.* Boston Studies in the Philosophy of Science, Volume I. 1963.
7. A. A. Zinov'ev, *Philosophical Problems of Many-Valued Logic.* 1963.
8. Georges Gurvitch, *The Spectrum of Social Time.* 1964.
9. Paul Lorenzen, *Formal Logic.* 1965.
10. Robert S. Cohen and Marx W. Wartofsky (eds.), *In Honor of Philipp Frank.* Boston Studies in the Philosophy of Science, Volume II. 1965.
11. Evert W. Beth, *Mathematical Thought. An Introduction to the Philosophy of Mathematics.* 1965.
12. Evert W. Beth and Jean Piaget, *Mathematical Epistemology and Psychology.* 1966.
13. Guido Küng, *Ontology and the Logistic Analysis of Language. An Enquiry into the Contemporary Views on Universals.* 1967.
14. Robert S. Cohen and Marx W. Wartofsky (eds.), *Proceedings of the Boston Colloquium for the Philosophy of Science 1964-1966. In Memory of Norwood Russell Hanson.* Boston Studies in the Philosophy of Science, Volume III. 1967.
15. C. D. Broad, *Induction, Probability, and Causation. Selected Papers.* 1968.
16. Günther Patzig, *Aristotle's Theory of the Syllogism. A Logical-Philosophical Study of Book A of the Prior Analytics.* 1968.
17. Nicholas Rescher, *Topics in Philosophical Logic.* 1968.
18. Robert S. Cohen and Marx W. Wartofsky (eds.), *Proceedings of the Boston Colloquium for the Philosophy of Science 1966-1968.* Boston Studies in the Philosophy of Science, Volume IV. 1969.

19. Robert S. Cohen and Marx W. Wartofsky (eds.), *Proceedings of the Boston Colloquium for the Philosophy of Science 1966-1968*. Boston Studies in the Philosophy of Science, Volume V. 1969.
20. J. W. Davis, D. J. Hockney, and W. K. Wilson (eds.), *Philosophical Logic*. 1969.
21. D. Davidson and J. Hintikka (eds.), *Words and Objections. Essays on the Work of W. V. Quine*. 1969.
22. Patrick Suppes, *Studies in the Methodology and Foundations of Science. Selected Papers from 1911 to 1969*. 1969.
23. Jaakko Hintikka, *Models for Modalities. Selected Essays*. 1969.
24. Nicholas Rescher *et al.* (eds.), *Essays in Honor of Carl G. Hempel. A Tribute on the Occasion of His Sixty-Fifth Birthday*. 1969.
25. P. V. Tavanec (ed.), *Problems of the Logic of Scientific Knowledge*. 1969.
26. Marshall Swain (ed.), *Induction, Acceptance, and Rational Belief*. 1970.
27. Robert S. Cohen and Raymond J. Seeger (eds.), *Ernst Mach: Physicist and Philosopher*. Boston Studies in the Philosophy of Science, Volume VI. 1970.
28. Jaakko Hintikka and Patrick Suppes, *Information and Inference*. 1970.
29. Karel Lambert, *Philosophical Problems in Logic. Some Recent Developments*. 1970.
30. Rolf A. Eberle, *Nominalistic Systems*. 1970.
31. Paul Weingartner and Gerhard Zecha (eds.), *Induction, Physics, and Ethics*. 1970.
32. Evert W. Beth, *Aspects of Modern Logic*. 1970.
33. Risto Hilpinen (ed.), *Deontic Logic: Introductory and Systematic Readings*. 1971.
34. Jean-Louis Krivine, *Introduction to Axiomatic Set Theory*. 1971.
35. Joseph D. Sneed, *The Logical Sstructure of Mathematical Physics*. 1971.
36. Carl R. Kordig, *The Justification of Scientific Change*. 1971.
37. Milic Capek, *Bergson and Modern Physics*. Boston Studies in the Philosophy of Science, Volume VII. 1971.
38. Norwood Russell Hanson, *What I Do Not Believe, and Other Essays* (ed. by Stephen Toulmin and Harry Woolf). 1971.
39. Roger C. Buck and Robert S. Cohen (eds.), *PSA 1970. In Memory of Rudolf Carnap*. Boston Studies in the Philosophy of Science, Volume VIII. 1971.
40. Donald Davidson and Gilbert Harman (eds.), *Semantics of Natural Language*. 1972.
41. Yehoshua Bar-Hillel (ed.), *Pragmatics of Natural Languages*. 1971.
42. Sören Stenlund, *Combinators, λ-Terms and Proof Theory*. 1972.
43. Martin Strauss, *Modern Physics and Its Philosophy. Selected Papers in the Logic, History, and Philosophy of Science*. 1972.
44. Mario Bunge, *Method, Model and Matter*. 1973.
45. Mario Bunge, *Philosophy of Physics*. 1973.
46. A. A. Zinov'ev, *Foundations of the Logical Theory of Scientific Knowledge (Complex Logic)*. (Revised and enlarged English edition with an appendix by G. A. Smirnov, E. A. Sidorenka, A. M. Fedina, and L. A. Bobrova.) Boston Studies in the Philosophy of Science, Volume IX. 1973.
47. Ladislav Tondl, *Scientific Procedures*. Boston Studies in the Philosophy of Science, Volume X. 1973.
48. Norwood Russell Hanson, *Constellations and Conjectures* (ed. by Willard C. Humphreys, Jr.). 1973.

49. K. J. J. Hintikka, J. M. E. Moravcsik, and P. Suppes (eds.), *Approaches to Natural Language*. 1973.
50. Mario Bunge (ed.), *Exact Philosophy – Problems, Tools, and Goals*. 1973.
51. Radu J. Bogdan and Ilkka Niiniluoto (eds.), *Logic, Language, and Probability*. 1973.
52. Glenn Pearce and Patrick Maynard (eds.), *Conceptual Change*. 1973.
53. Ilkka Niiniluoto and Raimo Tuomela, *Theoretical Concepts and Hypothetico-Inductive Inference*. 1973.
54. Roland Fraissé, *Course of Mathematical Logic* – Volume 1: *Relation and Logical Formula*. 1973.
55. Adolf Grünbaum, *Philosophical Problems of Space and Time*. (Second, enlarged edition.) Boston Studies in the Philosophy of Science, Volume XII. 1973.
56. Patrick Suppes (ed.), *Space, Time, and Geometry*. 1973.
57. Hans Kelsen, *Essays in Legal and Moral Philosophy* (selected and introduced by Ota Weinberger). 1973.
58. R. J. Seeger and Robert S. Cohen (eds.), *Philosophical Foundations of Science*. Boston Studies in the Philosophy of Science, Volume XI. 1974.
59. Robert S. Cohen and Marx W. Wartofsky (eds.), *Logical and Epistemological Studies in Contemporary Physics*. Boston Studies in the Philosophy of Science, Volume XIII. 1973.
60. Robert S. Cohen and Marx W. Wartofsky (eds.), *Methodological and Historical Essays in the Natural and Social Sciences. Proceedings of the Boston Colloquium for the Philosophy of Science 1969-1972*. Boston Studies in the Philosophy of Science, Volume XIV. 1974.
61. Robert S. Cohen, J. J. Stachel, and Marx W. Wartofsky (eds.), *For Dirk Struik. Scientific, Historical and Political Essays in Honor of Dirk J. Struik*. Boston Studies in the Philosophy of Science, Volume XV. 1974.
62. Kazimierz Ajdukiewicz, *Pragmatic Logic* (transl. from the Polish by Olgierd Wojtasiewicz). 1974.
63. Sören Stenlund (ed.), *Logical Theory and Semantic Analysis. Essays Dedicated to Stig Kanger on His Fiftieth Birthday*. 1974.
64. Kenneth F. Schaffner and Robert S. Cohen (eds.), *Proceedings of the 1972 Biennial Meeting, Philosophy of Science Association*. Boston Studies in the Philosophy of Science, Volume XX. 1974.
65. Henry E. Kyburg, Jr., *The Logical Foundations of Statistical Inference*. 1974.
66. Marjorie Grene, *The Understanding of Nature. Essays in the Philosophy of Biology*. Boston Studies in the Philosophy of Science, Volume XXIII. 1974.
67. Jan M. Broekman, *Structuralism: Moscow, Prague, Paris*. 1974.
68. Norman Geschwind, *Selected Papers on Language and the Brain*. Boston Studies in the Philosophy of Science, Volume XVI. 1974.
69. Roland Fraissé, *Course of Mathematical Logic* – Volume 2: *Model Theory*. 1974.
70. Andrzej Grzegorczyk, *An Outline of Mathematical Logic. Fundamental Results and Notions Explained with All Details*. 1974.
71. Franz von Kutschera, *Philosophy of Language*. 1975.
72. Juha Manninen and Raimo Tuomela (eds.), *Essays on Explanation and Understanding. Studies in the Foundations of Humanities and Social Sciences*. 1976.

73. Jaakko Hintikka (ed.), *Rudolf Carnap, Logical Empiricist. Materials and Perspectives.* 1975.
74. Milic Capek (ed.), *The Concepts of Space and Time. Their Structure and Their Development.* Boston Studies in the Philosophy of Science, Volume XXII. 1976.
75. Jaakko Hintikka and Unto Remes, *The Method of Analysis. Its Geometrical Origin and Its General Significance.* Boston Studies in the Philosophy of Science, Volume XXV. 1974.
76. John Emery Murdoch and Edith Dudley Sylla, *The Cultural Context of Medieval Learning.* Boston Studies in the Philosophy of Science, Volume XXVI. 1975.
77. Stefan Amsterdamski, *Between Experience and Metaphysics. Philosophical Problems of the Evolution of Science.* Boston Studies in the Philosophy of Science, Volume XXXV. 1975.
78. Patrick Suppes (ed.), *Logic and Probability in Quantum Mechanics.* 1976.
79. Hermann von Helmholtz: *Epistemological Writings. The Paul Hertz/Moritz Schlick Centenary Edition of 1921 with Notes and Commentary by the Editors.* (Newly translated by Malcolm F. Lowe. Edited, with an Introduction and Bibliography, by Robert S. Cohen and Yehuda Elkana.) Boston Studies in the Philosophy of Science, Volume XXXVII. 1977.
80. Joseph Agassi, *Science in Flux.* Boston Studies in the Philosophy of Science, Volume XXVIII. 1975.
81. Sandra G. Harding (ed.), *Can Theories Be Refuted? Essays on the Duhem-Quine Thesis.* 1976.
82. Stefan Nowak, *Methodology of Sociological Research. General Problems.* 1977.
83. Jean Piaget, Jean-Blaise Grize, Alina Szeminska, and Vinh Bang, *Epistemology and Psychology of Functions.* 1977.
84. Marjorie Grene and Everett Mendelsohn (eds.), *Topics in the Philosophy of Biology.* Boston Studies in the Philosophy of Science, Volume XXVII. 1976.
85. E. Fischbein, *The Intuitive Sources of Probabilistic Thinking in Children.* 1975.
86. Ernest W. Adams, *The Logic of Conditionals. An Application of Probability to Deductive Logic.* 1975.
87. Marian Przelecki and Ryszard Wójcicki (eds.), *Twenty-Five Years of Logical Methodology in Poland.* 1977.
88. J. Topolski, *The Methodology of History.* 1976.
89. A. Kasher (ed.), *Language in Focus: Foundations, Methods and Systems. Essays Dedicated to Yehoshua Bar-Hillel.* Boston Studies in the Philosophy of Science, Volume XLIII. 1976.
90. Jaakko Hintikka, *The Intentions of Intentionality and Other New Models for Modalities.* 1975.
91. Wolfgang Stegmüller, *Collected Papers on Epistemology, Philosophy of Science and History of Philosophy.* 2 Volumes. 1977.
92. Dov M. Gabbay, *Investigations in Modal and Tense Logics with Applications to Problems in Philosophy and Linguistics.* 1976.
93. Radu J. Bogdan, *Local Induction.* 1976.
94. Stefan Nowak, *Understanding and Prediction. Essays in the Methodology of Social and Behavioral Theories.* 1976.
95. Peter Mittelstaedt, *Philosophical Problems of Modern Physics.* Boston Studies in the Philosophy of Science, Volume XVIII. 1976.

96. Gerald Holton and William Blanpied (eds.), *Science and Its Public: The Changing Relationship.* Boston Studies in the Philosophy of Science, Volume XXXIII. 1976.
97. Myles Brand and Douglas Walton (eds.), *Action Theory.* 1976.
98. Paul Gochet, *Outline of a Nominalist Theory of Proposition. An Essay in the Theory of Meaning.* 1980.
99. R. S. Cohen, P. K. Feyerabend, and M. W. Wartofsky (eds.), *Essays in Memory of Imre Lakatos.* Boston Studies in the Philosophy of Science, Volume XXXIX. 1976.
100. R. S. Cohen and J. J. Stachel (eds.), *Selected Papers of Léon Rosenfeld.* Boston Studies in the Philosophy of Science, Volume XXI. 1978.
101. R. S. Cohen, C. A. Hooker, A. C. Michalos, and J. W. van Evra (eds.), *PSA 1974: Proceedings of the 1974 Biennial Meeting of the Philosophy of Science Association.* Boston Studies in the Philosophy of Science, Volume XXXII. 1976.
102. Yehuda Fried and Joseph Agassi, *Paranoia: A Study in Diagnosis.* Boston Studies in the Philosophy of Science, Volume L. 1976.
103. Marian Przelecki, Klemens Szaniawski, and Ryszard Wójcicki (eds.), *Formal Methods in the Methodology of Empirical Sciences.* 1976.
104. John M. Vickers, *Belief and Probability.* 1976.
105. Kurt H. Wolff, *Surrender and Catch: Experience and Inquiry Today.* Boston Studies in the Philosophy of Science, Volume LI. 1976.
106. Karel Kosík, *Dialectics of the Concrete.* Boston Studies in the Philosophy of Science, Volume LII. 1976.
107. Nelson Goodman, *The Structure of Appearance.* (Third edition.) Boston Studies in the Philosophy of Science, Volume LIII. 1977.
108. Jerzy Giedymin (ed.), *Kazimierz Ajdukiewicz: The Scientific World-Perspective and Other Essays, 1931-1963.* 1978.
109. Robert L. Causey, *Unity of Science.* 1977.
110. Richard E. Grandy, *Advanced Logic for Applications.* 1977.
111. Robert P. McArthur, *Tense Logic.* 1976.
112. Lars Lindahl, *Position and Change. A Study in Law and Logic.* 1977.
113. Raimo Tuomela, *Dispositions.* 1978.
114 Herbert A. Simon, *Models of Discovery and Other Topics in the Methods of Science.* Boston Studies in the Philosophy of Science, Volume LIV. 1977.
115. Roger D. Rosenkrantz, *Inference, Method and Decision.* 1977.
116. Raimo Tuomela, *Human Action and Its Explanation. A Study on the Philosophical Foundations of Psychology.* 1977.
117. Morris Lazerowitz, *The Language of Philosophy. Freud and Wittgenstein.* Boston Studies in the Philosophy of Science, Volume LV. 1977.
118. Stanislaw Leśniewski, *Collected Works* (ed. by S. J. Surma, J. T. J. Srzednicki, and D. I. Barnett, with an annotated bibliography by V. Frederick Rickey). 1982. (Forthcoming.)
119. Jerzy Pelc, *Semiotics in Poland, 1894-1969.* 1978.
120. Ingmar Pörn, *Action Theory and Social Science. Some Formal Models.* 1977.
121. Joseph Margolis, *Persons and Minds. The Prospects of Nonreductive Materialism.* Boston Studies in the Philosophy of Science, Volume LVII. 1977.
122. Jaakko Hintikka, Ilkka Niiniluoto, and Esa Saarinen (eds.), *Essays on Mathematical and Philosophical Logic.* 1978.
123. Theo A. F. Kuipers, *Studies in Inductive Probability and Rational Expectation.* 1978.

124. Esa Saarinen, Risto Hilpinen, Ilkka Niiniluoto, and Merrill Provence Hintikka (eds.), *Essays in Honour of Jaakko Hintikka on the Occasion of His Fiftieth Birthday*. 1978.
125 Gerard Radnitzky and Gunnar Andersson (eds.), *Progress and Rationality in Science*. Boston Studies in the Philosophy of Science, Volume LVIII. 1978.
126. Peter Mittelstaedt, *Quantum Logic*. 1978.
127. Kenneth A. Bowen, *Model Theory for Modal Logic. Kripke Models for Modal Predicate Calculi*. 1978.
128. Howard Alexander Bursen, *Dismantling the Memory Machine. A Philosophical Investigation of Machine Theories of Memory*. 1978.
129. Marx W. Wartofsky, *Models: Representation and the Scientific Understanding*. Boston Studies in the Philosophy of Science, Volume XLVIII. 1979.
130. Don Ihde, *Technics and Praxis. A Philosophy of Technology*. Boston Studies in the Philosophy of Science, Volume XXIV. 1978.
131. Jerzy J. Wiatr (ed.), *Polish Essays in the Methodology of the Social Sciences*. Boston Studies in the Philosophy of Science, Volume XXIX. 1979.
132. Wesley C. Salmon (ed.), *Hans Reichenbach: Logical Empiricist*. 1979.
133. Peter Bieri, Rolf-P. Horstmann, and Lorenz Krüger (eds.), *Transcendental Arguments in Science. Essays in Epistemology*. 1979.
134. Mihailo Marković and Gajo Petrović (eds.), *Praxis. Yugoslav Essays in the Philosophy and Methodology of the Social Sciences*. Boston Studies in the Philosophy of Science, Volume XXXVI. 1979.
135. Ryszard Wójcicki, *Topics in the Formal Methodology of Empirical Sciences*. 1979.
136. Gerard Radnitzky and Gunnar Andersson (eds.), *The Structure and Development of Science*. Boston Studies in the Philosophy of Science, Volume LIX. 1979.
137. Judson Chambers Webb. *Mechanism, Mentalism, and Metamathematics. An Essay on Finitism*. 1980.
138. D. F. Gustafson and B. L. Tapscott (eds.), *Body, Mind, and Method. Essays in Honor of Virgil C. Aldrich*. 1979.
139. Leszek Nowak, *The Structure of Idealization. Towards a Systematic Interpretation of the Marxian Idea of Science*. 1979.
140. Chaim Perelman, *The New Rhetoric and the Humanities. Essays on Rhetoric and Its Applications*. 1979.
141. Wlodzimierz Rabinowicz, *Universalizability. A Study in Morals and Metaphysics*. 1979.
142. Chaim Perelman, *Justice, Law, and Argument. Essays on Moral and Legal Reasoning*. 1980.
143. Stig Kanger and Sven Öhman (eds.), *Philosophy and Grammar. Papers on the Occasion of the Quincentennial of Uppsala University*. 1981.
144. Tadeusz Pawlowski, *Concept Formation in the Humanities and the Social Sciences*. 1980.
145. Jaakko Hintikka, David Gruender, and Evandro Agazzi (eds.), *Theory Change, Ancient Axiomatics, and Galileo's Methodology. Proceedings of the 1978 Pisa Conference on the History and Philosophy of Science, Volume I*. 1981.
146. Jaakko Hintikka, David Gruender, and Evandro Agazzi (eds.), *Probabilistic Thinking, Thermodynamics, and the Interaction of the History and Philosophy of*

Science. Proceedings of the 1978 Pisa Conference on the History and Philosophy of Science, Volume II. 1981.
147. Uwe Mönnich (ed.), *Aspects of Philosophical Logic. Some Logical Forays into Central Notions of Linguistics and Philosophy.* 1981.
148. Dov M. Gabbay, *Semantical Investigations in Heyting's Intuitionistic Logic.* 1981.
149. Evandro Agazzi (ed.), *Modern Logic – A Survey. Historical, Philosophical, and Mathematical Aspects of Modern Logic and its Applications.* 1981.
150. A. F. Parker-Rhodes, *The Theory of Indistinguishables. A Search for Explanatory Principles below the Level of Physics.* 1981.
151. J. C. Pitt, *Pictures, Images, and Conceptual Change. An Analysis of Wilfrid Sellars' Philosophy of Science.* 1981.
152. R. Hilpinen (ed.), *New Studies in Deontic Logic. Norms, Actions, and the Foundations of Ethics.* 1981.
153. C. Dilworth, *Scientific Progress. A Study Concerning the Nature of the Relation Between Successive Scientific Theories.* 1981.
154. D. W. Smith and R. McIntyre, *Husserl and Intentionality. A Study of Mind, Meaning, and Language.* 1982.
155. R. J. Nelson, *The Logic of Mind.* 1982.
156. J. F. A. K. van Benthem, *The Logic of Time. A Model-Theoretic Investigation into the Varieties of Temporal Ontology, and Temporal Discourse.* 1982.
157. R. Swinburne (ed.), *Space, Time and Causality.* 1982.
158. R. D. Rozenkrantz, *E. T. Jaynes: Papers on Probability, Statistics and Statistical Physics.* 1983.
159. T. Chapman, *Time: A Philosophical Analysis.* 1982.
160. E. N. Zalta, *Abstract Objects. An Introduction to Axiomatic Metaphysics.* 1983.
161. S. Harding and M. B. Hintikka (eds.), *Discovering Reality. Feminist Perspectives on Epistemology, Metaphysics, Methodology, and Philosophy of Science.* 1983.
162. M. A. Stewart (ed.), *Law, Morality and Rights.* 1983.
163. D. Mayr and G. Süssmann (eds.), *Space, Time, and Mechanics. Basic Structures of a Physical Theory.* 1983.
164. D. M. Gabbay and F. Guenther (eds.), *Handbook of Philosophical Logic,* Volume I. 1983, forthcoming.
165. D. M. Gabbay and F. Guenther (eds.), *Handbook of Philosophical Logic,* Volume II. 1983, forthcoming.
166. D. M. Gabbay and F. Guenther (eds.), *Handbook of Philosophical Logic,* Volume III. 1983, forthcoming.
167. D. M. Gabbay and F. Guenther (eds.), *Handbook of Philosophical Logic,* Volume IV. 1983, forthcoming.